TEST YOUR BIBLE I.Q.

TEST YOUR BIBLE I.Q.

1,000
Bible Questions
and Answers

CATHY DRINKWATER BETTER

TESTAMENT
BOOKS

New York

This 2000 edition is published by Testament Books,™ an imprint of Random House
Value Publishing, Inc., 280 Park Avenue, New York, NY 10017, by arrangement with
Ottenheimer Publishers, Inc., 5 Park Center Court, Suite 300,
Owings Mills, MD 21117

Testament Books™ and design are trademarks of
Random House Value Publishing, Inc.

Random House
New York • Toronto • London • Sydney • Auckland
http://www.randomhouse.com/

Printed and bound in the United States of America.

Library of Congress Cataloging-in-Publication Data

Better, Cathy Drinkwater.
        Test your Bible I.Q. : 1,000 Bible questions and answers / Cathy
Drinkwater Better.
                p.   cm.
        ISBN 0-517-16097-8
        1. Bible--Miscellanea. 1. Title.   II. Title: Test your Bible I.Q.
        BS612.B48   1999   220-dc21
                                                                        98-56181
                                                                            CIP

ISBN 0-517-16097-8
                        8 7 6 5 4 3 2

TABLE
OF
CONTENTS

INTRODUCTION

There has never been another book to compare with
the Bible. Really a collection of sixty-six separate
books written by some forty different authors, the
Bible brings us law and history, poetry and song,
heroes and villains, prophecy, prayer, miracles, and
stories as exciting as any novel ever written. The Bible
has changed the course of civilization and given the
human spirit a clear vision of heaven. It can make us
weep, lead us to ponder, or fill our hearts with joy
and hope.

The very first books of the Bible were written millen-
nia ago; yet the same teachings that have enlightened
and inspired readers for thousands of years are still
alive for us today, as fresh and as relevant as ever. The
Old and New Testaments form a blueprint for a
happy and spiritually fulfilling life. But how well do
you know this age-old "Book of Books"?

Test Your Bible I.Q. is an enjoyable and informative way to test your knowledge of Bible scripture. Basic factual questions, quizzes, puzzles, and trivia games illuminate the Bible from Genesis to Revelation. The questions are numbered from one to one thousand to help you keep track of your progress, and the answers, each with an accompanying scriptural reference, appear at the back of the book. Special "extra credit" boxes called "Bible Brain Busters" are scattered throughout to bring Bible people, places, and things into sharper focus while offering you additional challenge. All scriptural quotations are taken from the King James Version of the Bible.

Use this book to get more out of Bible study groups, to develop exciting quizzes for Bible classes, or to start meaningful family discussions. Amaze your friends with Bible trivia. Take *Test Your Bible I.Q.* along on family trips for hours of fascinating "Q-and-A" that will make the miles fly by. Or just have fun while boosting your own understanding of the Scriptures.

There is no more personally or spiritually rewarding pastime than increasing your knowledge of the Bible and all it has to offer. Why not see how you stack up when it comes to Bible know-how? Grab a pencil, a pad of paper, and your trusty, well-worn Bible, and *Test Your Bible I.Q.*

Good luck, have fun . . . and no peeking!

CHAPTER 1

Warm-Up: Flexing Your Bible Trivia Muscles

Here are some relatively easy questions about the Bible, just to get you started. Ready, set . . . GO!

1. From what did God create Adam, the first man?
2. This rained from the sky when God destroyed Sodom and Gomorrah.
3. Who said, "Repent ye, for the kingdom of heaven is at hand"?
4. Jesus compared the kingdom of God to what tiny object?
5. What happened to keep the lions from harming Daniel?
6. Who did Moses anoint with ram's blood?
7. Jesus sent this man to catch a fish that held a coin in its mouth.
8. Who said, "The Lord gave, and the Lord hath taken away; blessed be the name of the Lord?"

9. Upon what "rock" did Jesus build his church?
10. Where did Jonah go to board a ship bound for Tarshish?
11. Of ten lepers Jesus healed, how many thanked him?
12. Finish this Bible verse: "Pride goeth before _____, and _____ before a fall."

BIBLE BRAIN BUSTER

Match each Bible word to its meaning.

1. woman	a. vision or revelation
2. Babel	b. taken out of man
3. Bethel	c. booths
4. Succoth	d. elder
5. Legion	e. worldly riches
6. trespass	f. House of God
7. Eden	g. many
8. cleave	h. delight
9. vinegar	i. a debt
10. dowry	j. bride price
11. priest	k. friendship
12. Hebron	l. remain faithful
13. apostle	m. a sour wine drink
14. mammon	n. confusion
15. Apocalypse	o. messenger, one who is sent

Answers: 1. b, 2. n, 3. f, 4. c, 5. g, 6. i, 7. h, 8. l, 9. m, 10. j, 11. d, 12. k, 13. o, 14. e, 15. a

13. She was Moses' first wife.
14. Who refused to leave her mother-in-law, saying, ". . . for whither thou goest, I will go; and where thou lodgest, I will lodge: thy people shall be my people, and thy God my God"?
15. Why did Zacchaeus, the tax collector, have to climb a tree to see Jesus?
16. Who went forth to meet his enemy without armor, carrying only a staff, a sling, and five smooth stones?
17. Complete this Bible verse: "Blessed are the pure in heart, _____."
18. What wise king suggested that a baby be divided in two to settle an argument?
19. In Revelation, which horse represents Death?
20. The sixth commandment prohibits what act?
21. How many plagues did God send down upon Egypt before Pharaoh allowed the Israelites to leave?
22. According to Proverbs, a lazy man should look to this insect for inspiration.
23. How did Isaiah know that his sins had been forgiven?
24. What did God give as a sign of his promise to never again destroy the earth by flood?
25. What psalm compares the way God cares for us to the way a shepherd cares for his flock?

BIBLE BRAIN BUSTER

Which Bible verses gave us these everyday expressions?

1. A wolf in sheep's clothing
2. A leopard doesn't change its spots.
3. A drop in the bucket
4. The salt of the earth
5. By the skin of my teeth

6. Eat, drink and be merry!
7. The fat of the land
8. The blind leading the blind

Answers: 1. Matthew 7:15, 2. Jeremiah 13:23, 3. Isaiah 40:15, 4. Matthew 5:13, 5. Job 19:20, 6. Ecclesiastes 8:15, 7. Genesis 45:18, 8. Matthew 15:14

26. Who was the first of Jesus' twelve apostles?
27. With God's help, who interpreted King Nebuchadnezzar's dream?
28. Which judge fathered seventy sons?
29. His wife was turned into a pillar of salt.
30. What runaway slave was the subject of one of Paul's epistles?
31. When this man's father gave him a welcoming home party, his brother became angry.
32. Who suggested that Jesus turn stones into bread?
33. Where did the angel tell Joseph to take Mary and the baby Jesus to escape King Herod's anger?

34. Who said, "I find no fault in this man"?
35. Who sold his birthright for a helping of stew?
36. Aeneas was paralyzed. Who healed him?
37. Who rescued Lot and his family from the destruction of Sodom?
38. This prophet predicted that the Messiah would come riding on a donkey.
39. How did David make an evil spirit leave Saul?
40. After the Resurrection, Jesus proved that he was not an apparition by eating this.
41. Who tore his clothing upon hearing that all of his sons and daughters had died at once?
42. What king killed himself by falling upon his sword?
43. How did Joseph know to name his son Jesus?
44. Who will open the book with seven seals?
45. Who sent birds flying from the window of a boat?
46. This married woman was the object of David's affection.
47. Besides Isaiah, what Old Testament prophet saw the Lord sitting upon a throne?
48. She was Ruth's sister-in-law.
49. Where did Jesus sit to speak with a sinful woman?
50. Why was manna placed in the ark of the covenant?

Now, check your answers starting on page 131. How well did you do? Are you ready for more challenging fare? Read on!

CHAPTER 2

People in the Bible

Who Was It?

51. Sold into slavery by his brothers
52. Stoned to death
53. Taken to heaven in a whirlwind
54. Planted the first garden
55. Devoured by fire for an improper offering to the Lord
56. Fortified Jerusalem
57. Helped spies escape through a window
58. Father of the Jewish nation
59. Evicted from their home for disobedience
60. A blind beggar healed by Jesus
61. Said, "Lord, lay not this sin to their charge"
62. Caused a riot at Ephesus
63. Peter's brother, an apostle
64. Began the rebuilding of the temple
65. A governor of Jerusalem who helped rebuild it

BIBLE BRAIN BUSTER

Match these biblical names with their meanings.

1. Zachariah		a.	admired, praised
2. John		b.	innocent
3. Abraham		c.	the captivator
4. Sarah		d.	princess
5. Rachel		e.	high mountain
6. Joshua		f.	breath
7. David		g.	man of earth
8. Daniel		h.	the Lord is judge
9. Gabriel		i.	beloved
10. Abel		j.	God is with us
11. Rebekah		k.	God's strength
12. Aaron		l.	God is mighty
13. Peter		m.	the supplanter
14. Samuel		n.	God's gracious gift
15. Judith		o.	whom God has saved
16. Emmanuel		p.	rock
17. Jacob		q.	sun-like
18. Ezekiel		r.	name of God
19. Adam		s.	the Lord's remembrance
20. Samson		t.	father of many

Answers: 1. s, 2. n, 3. t, 4. d, 5. b, 6. o, 7. i, 8. k, 9. l, 10. f, 11. c, 12. e, 13. p, 14. r, 15. a, 16. j, 17. m, 18. h, 19. g, 20. q

66. Asked Jesus to heal his dying daughter
67. Prayed from inside a fish

68. On God's orders, married a harlot named Gomer
69. Invited a king to dinner
70. Preached against divorce
71. Carried the cross for Jesus on the day he was crucified
72. Disciple who doubted Christ's resurrection
73. Spoke to Pharaoh for Moses
74. The sister of Mary and Lazarus
75. Helped Esther save the Jews
76. With Aaron, held up Moses' arms during the battle of Amalek
77. Paid to discover the secret of Samson's strength
78. Had put blessings in his mouth by God
79. Built the first temple
80. Asked for Jesus' body and laid it in the tomb
81. Became king at the age of eight
82. Sent to Antioch with Paul and Barnabus
83. An evil man promoted by King Ahasuerus
84. Adam and Eve's second son
85. The mother of John the Baptist
86. Emperor of Rome when Jesus was born
87. Raised from the dead by Peter
88. Joseph's Egyptian master
89. Wrote a prayer that might have been intended for a temple orchestra
90. Jesus' brother
91. Born to the aged Abraham and Sarah

BIBLE BRAIN BUSTER

Unscramble these Bible names.

1. HOENC
2. SUMLEEHAHT
3. TANHNELAA
4. LPIHPI
5. BAAMHRA

6. DOMARECI
7. AHM
8. WHATETM
9. AJSUD
10. HOIBADA

Answers: 1. Enoch, 2. Methuselah, 3. Nathanael, 4. Philip, 5. Abraham, 6. Mordecai, 7. Ham, 8. Matthew, 9. Judas, 10. Obadiah.

92. Prophesied to those exiled in Mesopotamia
93. The last great judge of Israel, a prophet
94. The sister of Moses and Aaron
95. Married to Boaz, Jesus' non-Jewish ancestor
96. Made king over Judah and Jerusalem by Nebuchadnezzar
97. Helped David reconcile with his son, Absalom
98. The daughter of Jacob and Leah
99. Released to the people instead of Jesus
100. Murdered his own brother
101. Born holding onto his brother's heel
102. "The Zealot," an apostle
103. A great help to Paul in his missionary work
104. Hated John the Baptist because he said it was unlawful for a man to marry his brother's wife

105. Worshiped Baal to please his wife

Who Said That?

106. "The Lord is slow to anger and great in power."
107. "The Lord bless thee and keep thee; the Lord make His face shine upon thee, and be gracious unto thee; the Lord lift up His countenance upon thee, and give thee peace."
108. "Wisdom is better than rubies."
109. "God loveth a cheerful giver."
110. "Whatsoever a man soweth, that shall he also reap."
111. "My breath is corrupt, and my days are extinct, the graves are ready for me."
112. "Therefore their goods shall become a booty, and their houses a desolation; they shall also build houses, but not inhabit them; and they shall plant vineyards, but not drink the wine thereof."
113. "Thou couldest have no power at all against me, except it were given thee from above."
114. "And I saw a new heaven and a new earth, for the first heaven and the first earth were passed away; and there was no more sea."
115. "Ye shall not surely die."

BIBLE BRAIN BUSTER

Bible ABC's: Name these Bible people from A to Z.

David's son; he tried to usurp his father's throne:
A_____

This Jewish Christian traveled with Paul: B_____

A high priest; he played a role in Jesus' trial:
C_____

She was paid to discover the secret of Samson's strength: D_____

He was Jacob's hairy twin: E_____

He presided over Paul's trial at Caesarea:
F_____

This celebrated judge of Israel delivered his people from the Midianites: G_____

During the battle with Amalek, he was one of the men who held up Moses' arms: H_____

The son born to Abraham and Sarah in their old age: I_____

His job was to prepare the way for the Messiah:
J_____

This Levite took a foreign wife: K_____

He escaped from Sodom, but his wife was not so lucky: L_____

He helped Esther save the Jews: M_____

This pharisee assisted in Jesus' burial:
N_____

Paul defended this Christian slave in a letter to Philemon: O_____

BIBLE BRAIN BUSTER

Bible ABC's: Name these Bible people from A to Z. (continued)

Captain of the guard, he was Joseph's Egyptian master: P_____

Paul sent greetings from this Christian to the Romans: Q_____

She was the mother of Jacob and Esau: R_____

"The Zealot," he was one of Jesus' twelve apostles: S_____

Another one of the twelve apostles, he initially doubted Jesus' resurrection: T_____

This son of Abinadab was killed miraculously for touching the ark of God: U_____

Her husband, the king, divorced her for refusing to attend his great feast: V_____

Also known as the Magi, these three visited the baby Jesus: W_____ _____

The king of Persia (also known as Ahasuerus): X_____

Helped Saul find Samuel: Y_____

Jesus visited this tax collector in Jericho: Z_____

Answers: Absalom, Barnabas, Caiaphas, Delilah, Esau, Felix, Gideon, Hur, Isaac, John, Kelaiah, Lot, Mordecai, Nicodemus, Onesimus, Potiphar, Quartus, Rebekah, Simon, Thomas, Uzzah, Vashti, wise men, Xerxes, young maidens, Zacchaeus

116. "Although all shall be offended, yet will not I."

117. "For what is a man advantaged, if he gain the whole world, and lose himself, or be cast away?"

118. "As the lily among thorns, so is my love among the daughters."

119. "This stone, which I have set for a pillar, shall be God's house; and of all that thou shalt give me I will surely give the tenth unto thee."

120. "Faith without works is dead."

121. "Turn from thy fierce wrath, and repent of this evil against thy people."

122. "This is the bread which the Lord hath given you to eat."

123. "I set my face unto the Lord God, to seek by prayer and supplications, with fasting, and sackcloth, and ashes."

124. "As I was with Moses, so I will be with thee. I will not fail thee, nor forsake thee."

125. "Lord, if it be thou, bid me come unto thee on the water."

126. "O my son Absalom! O Absalom, my son, my son!"

127. "Who is the Lord, that I should obey his voice to let Israel go?"

128. "I saw a dream which made me afraid, and the thoughts upon my bed and the visions of my head troubled me."

129. "Rabbi, we know that thou art a teacher come from God: for no man can do these miracles that thou doest, unless God be with him."

130. "I have need to be baptized of thee, and comest thou to me?"

131. "Behold, a virgin shall conceive, and bear a son, and shall call his name Immanuel."

132. "The serpent beguiled me, and I did eat."

133. "My punishment is greater than I can bear."

134. "How long halt ye between two opinions? If the Lord be God, follow him; but if Baal, then follow him."

135. "Repent, and be baptized every one of you in the name of Jesus Christ for the remission of sins."

136. "What shall be the sign that the Lord will heal me, and that I shall go up into the house of the Lord the third day?"

137. "This is one of the Hebrews' children."

138. "Behold the handmaid of the Lord."

139. "My father made your yoke heavy, and I will add to your yoke; my father also chastised you with whips, but I will chastise you with scorpions."

140. "Am I a dog, that thou comest to me with staves?"

141. "Turn again, my daughters: why will ye go with me? Are there yet any more sons in my womb, that they may be your husbands?"

142. "Shall I go and call to thee a nurse of the Hebrew women, that she may nurse the child for thee?"

143. "Treason, Treason!"

144. "This is John the Baptist; he is risen from the dead; and therefore mighty works do shew (show) forth themselves in him."

145. "We are all one man's sons; we are true men, thy servants are no spies."

BIBLE BRAIN BUSTER

There were many great Bible leaders, but there were also some very famous followers. Match each of these Bible people with who or what they followed.

1. Moses
2. Samson
3. Paul
4. The wise men
5. Peter
6. Joseph

a. a dream
b. a star
c. a pillar of cloud
d. a heavenly vision
e. a deceitful woman
f. an angel

Answers: 1. c (Numbers 10:33–34), 2. e (Judges 14:3), 3. d (Acts 16:9), 4. b (Matthew 2:2), 5. f (Acts 12:8), 6. a (Genesis 37:5, 9–10)

What's in a Name?

What were their *original* names?

146. Peter

147. Paul

148. Zedekiah

149. Abraham

150. Sarah

151. Solomon

152. Israel

153. Joshua

154. Jehoiakim

155. Belteshazzar

Husbands and Wives, Sons and Daughters

156. This wife of David was once married to Nabal.

157. She watched over her children's corpses to protect them from scavenging animals.

158. The Hittite wife of Esau

159. They were both wives of Lamech.

160. The husband of Judith, Bashemath, and Mahalath

161. This woman made her son a new coat each year when she went to make a sacrifice.

162. Jesus knew this woman had had five husbands.

163. He married Herodias even though her husband, his brother Herod Philip, was still alive.

164. Called "the bride of Christ"
165. This king of Judah had sixty daughters and twenty-eight sons.
166. This priest spoiled and indulged his sons.
167. He married the two sisters Leah and Rachel.
168. She was Joseph's Egyptian wife.
169. She married two sons of Judah.
170. Mordecai's adopted daughter
171. He was forced to live in a cave with his two daughters after his house was destroyed.
172. The nations of the earth were formed from his sons.
173. After three days, they found their lost son in the temple.
174. This daughter asked for John the Baptist's head on a platter to please her mother.
175. The son of Zerubbabel
176. She was Haruz's daughter, Manasseh's wife, and Amon's mother.
177. She was a daughter of Herod Agrippa I, and became wife to Felix, governor of Judea.
178. He was the father of at least two of David's valiant men.
179. He was Jacob's youngest son, whom Jacob was afraid to let go to Egypt for fear some harm would come to him.
180. She was the mother of Moses.

Bible Rulers

181. This son of Gideon was proclaimed king in Shechem.
182. Though he was at the point of death, this king had fifteen years added to his life because of his strong faith.
183. The youngest of eight sons, this shepherd boy was anointed by Samuel as his brothers looked on.
184. Jesus referred to this ruler as a "fox."
185. The judge Ehud murdered this overweight king of Moab.
186. What king made a covenant before the Lord?
187. A Hebrew captive, he interpreted the dreams of an Egyptian pharaoh.
188. This king had the prophet Urijah murdered for opposing him.
189. What king of the Amorites refused to allow the Israelites to travel through his kingdom?
190. This Roman ruler ordered a census to be taken in the empire.
191. What king fell through a lattice in his upper chamber?
192. When this king hosted a banquet, a phantom hand left a message on the palace wall.
193. This king of Gerar took Sarah away from Abraham.

BIBLE BRAIN BUSTER

Use the clues and rearrange the letters to form the name of these kings during the time of the prophets Elijah and Elisha.

1. ELAAZH (anointed by Elijah)
2. THOJEPHAAHS (built a fleet of merchant ships that never sailed)
3. AND-IBADEH (king of Aram)
4. ZIAHAAH (fell from an upper room)
5. SNIHIM (the father of King Jehu)
6. MEAJORH (the father of Jehosheba)

Answers: 1. Hazael, 2. Jehoshphat, 3. Ben-hadad, 4. Ahaziah, 5. Nimshi, 6. Jehoram

194. He ordered the infant sons of Bethlehem killed.

195. This queen visited King Solomon and was impressed by his great wisdom.

196. During the time of the judges, this Canaanite king was renowned for owning nine hundred iron chariots.

197. What king of Judah led his country into sin by marrying the wicked Ahab's daughter?

198. Who was king in Persia when Nehemiah heard that the wall of Jerusalem was broken down and the gate burned?

199. This evil king of Judah repented after being taken to Babylon in chains.
200. He gave his daughter Jezebel to be Ahab's wife.
201. What king of Israel was murdered while he was drunk?
202. He built an altar, asking for an end to a plague.
203. Which king executed John the Baptist to please his wife and stepdaughter?
204. God sent this king of Mesopotamia to conquer the faithless Israelites.
205. This king led Israel into sin by allowing his wife to introduce the worship of the false god Baal into the country.
206. This king dreamed that a huge, fruitful tree was suddenly chopped down, leaving only a stump.
207. Paul told the story of his conversion to this king.
208. He decreed the rebuilding of the temple.
209. This king pitched a javelin at David.
210. Which king of the Amalekites was captured by Saul and cut into pieces by Samuel?
211. Who was king when the Book of the Law was finally found?
212. When Jesus was arrested and brought to him, this king demanded to see miracles.
213. He promoted Haman to sit above all the other princes.

214. Which three kings listened to the prophet Elisha as he played his harp and prophesied?

215. This son of Jeroboam reigned for six months, and then was assassinated by Shallum.

216. He ordered Daniel thrown into the lions' den.

217. Which king was struck with leprosy for allowing his subjects to worship idols?

218. He was imprisoned by Assyria's King Shalmaneser.

219. He was mourned throughout Judah and Jerusalem after being mortally wounded during a battle in the valley of Megiddo.

220. He built the first temple in Jerusalem.

221. Which king authored the Song of Songs?

222. The prophet Nathan confronted this king about an adulterous affair.

223. This king refused to let the Israelites pass through his country on the way to Canaan.

224. Which king of Salem was also a priest of the most high God?

225. This king of Moab was also a sheep farmer.

226. He gave orders to have James executed and Peter arrested.

227. He was the last king of Judah.

228. This king of Bashan had an iron bed nine cubits long and four cubits wide.

229. The prophet Micaiah told this king that his troops would lose in battle.

230. Which ruler ordered a plaque attached to the cross proclaiming Jesus "King of the Jews"?

Women of the Bible

231. She hatched a plot to have John the Baptist executed by her husband, Herod.

232. Who died giving birth to Benjamin?

233. This widow praised God when she saw the baby Jesus.

234. She was Jacob's daughter, and she had twelve brothers.

235. She was married to the priest Zacharias.

236. Which woman asked Jesus for water he said would quench her thirst forever?

237. This harlot became a heroine when she helped save the lives of Joshua's spies.

238. Jesus cried when he found out their brother was dead.

239. Paul asked these two women to stop their quarreling.

240. Who was the Hittite wife of Esau?

241. She brought David and his men 200 loaves of bread after her husband had selfishly refused them food and shelter.

242. She was the first of Jacob's wives to bear a child.
243. Pretending to be a widow, she spoke to the king on Joab's behalf.
244. This widow's father-in-law mistook her for a harlot when she covered her face.
245. Who was the queen of Egypt during the reigns of David and Solomon?
246. What woman saved her people from extinction?
247. She falsely accused her Hebrew servant of trying to seduce her.
248. The wife of the soldier Uriah, she became David's wife and bore him a son, Solomon.
249. This prophetess could claim two great leaders as her brothers, and once suffered leprosy as a punishment for rebellion.
250. What Egyptian woman was the mother of two tribes of Israel?
251. What was the name of King Saul's wife?
252. Jesus told her, "I am the resurrection, and the life."
253. She danced so well for her stepfather, Herod, that he offered her anything she wanted.
254. This woman gave milk to an enemy soldier— and then killed him.
255. She was King Agrippa's companion.
256. This widow had two widowed daughters-in-law.

257. Mary's cousin, she conceived a child in her old age.

258. This woman was a widow—but only for about three hours.

259. She left her widowed mother-in-law and returned to her family.

260. Luke referred to this woman as a prophetess.

261. The only female judge of Israel, she judged from beneath a palm tree.

262. She was the mother of two of Jesus' disciples.

263. This loving mother lied and schemed to obtain a blessing for her favorite son.

264. Although King Saul decreed her profession illegal, still he disguised himself to seek her assistance.

265. This widow was thrown from a window by her servants after putting on makeup.

266. Which prophetess prophesied during the reign of Josiah?

267. According to the Bible, who were the first two women to share a husband?

268. What was the name of Sarah's Egyptian maid?

269. Jesus healed this woman of a fever.

270. She sat at Jesus' feet while her sister did the housework.

271. Who did King David see washing herself on a rooftop?

272. She was replaced on the throne by Esther.
273. She was queen of the Ethiopians.
274. She lost her power because she worshiped idols.
275. Saul's daughter, she was married to David.
276. She was the queen of Egypt.
277. These two women were the only females to have books of the Bible named after them.
278. She was chosen to be a wife for giving some camels some water.
279. She housed Paul at Philippi, relieving him of the necessity of earning a living so he could devote himself to God.
280. They were the first to see Jesus after the Resurrection.

Heroes and Villains

281. He obtained a royal decree allowing the persecution and extermination of the Jews.
282. He was stoned to death because he was a follower of Jesus.
283. Who brought a building crashing down upon himself in order to kill his enemies?
284. He was commanded by God to lead his people out of bondage in Egypt.
285. He wisely spearheaded a plan to store grain for the coming famine.

286. She used her influence on her husband to save her people from destruction.
287. This Israelite leader defeated six nations and thirty-one kings, but is best known for bringing the walls of a city tumbling down.
288. He sent the Philistine army running—after killing their champion soldier—while only a boy.
289. The prophet Elijah was forced to flee the wrath of this queen after he bested 450 prophets of Baal.
290. He betrayed a friend with a kiss (but later repented and hanged himself).

Bible Children

291. Who tricked his father into giving him a blessing that rightfully belonged to his brother?
292. Who killed his brother in a fit of rage?
293. What was the name of Noah's youngest son?
294. Rachel died giving birth to him.
295. Who was Joseph's youngest son?
296. In the Bible, who were the first twins mentioned?
297. What lesser-known judge had thirty sons?
298. Was the prodigal son older or younger than his brother?

299. This aptly named prophet in King David's court had fourteen sons and three daughters.

300. Whose wives gave him nineteen sons and one daughter?

301. Jesus cured this dying child.

302. Hannah gave up her son to do the Lord's work, in gratitude for his birth. What was his name?

303. This child shared information that led Naaman to be cured of leprosy.

304. This boy nearly became a sacrifice at the hands of his father, Abraham.

305. He spent his first night on earth sleeping in a manger.

Old and New Testament Prophets

Messianic prophets foretold the following New Testament events. Name the Old Testament book in which these prophecies appear:

306. The crucifixion of Jesus along with two thieves

307. That the Messiah would speak in parables

308. Jesus' birth in Bethlehem

309. That Jesus would be betrayed for thirty pieces of silver

310. That people would cast lots for Jesus' robe

311. That the Messiah would suffer in silence

BIBLE BRAIN BUSTER

The prophet Elijah and his disciple Elisha were two of the greatest Old Testament prophets. Can you tell one from the other?

1. He foretold that Ahaziah would die on his sickbed as a punishment for sending his messengers to inquire of Baal-zebub.
2. He used a bow and arrows to predict the future of Joash.
3. He fled to the wilderness when Jezebel wanted to kill him.
4. He was fed by ravens while in hiding.
5. Beneath a juniper tree, he prayed to die.
6. He told the Shunammite woman that she would have a son.
7. By multiplying her oil supply, he helped a widow whose sons were about to be taken from her by her creditors.
8. He used his mantel to divide the waters of the river Jordan.
9. The woman of Shunem built and furnished a special room for him.
10. With God's help, he cured a child by stretching himself over the boy three times and praying.

Answers: 1. Elijah (2 Kings 1:16–17), 2. Elisha (2 Kings 13:14–19), 3. Elijah (1 Kings 19:1–3) 4. Elijah (1 Kings 17:3–4), 5. Elijah (1 Kings 19:4), 6. Elisha (2 Kings 4:15–16), 37. Elisha (2 Kings 4:1–7), 8. Elijah (2 Kings 2:8), 9. Elisha (2 Kings 4:8–10) 10. Elijah (1 Kings 17:21)

312. That Jesus would enter Jerusalem on a donkey
313. That the Messiah would be a mighty prophet in word and deed
314. That Jesus' hands and feet would be pierced
315. That the Messiah would be rejected and despised
316. That the Messiah would be born of a virgin
317. That Jesus, Mary, and Joseph would leave Egypt and return to Galilee
318. The Resurrection
319. That the Messiah would be a sacrificial offering for mankind's sins
320. That Jesus' side would be pierced with a sword

Name the prophets described in the following questions.

321. Who was the successor of Elijah?
322. He spoke out against social injustice and unrighteousness.
323. This prophet opposed the worship of Baal at the time of Ahab and Jezebel.
324. Before the Flood, he prophesied about God's judgment against the sinners.
325. He declared God's forgiveness and love for the faithless Israelites.
326. This prophet foretold the siege of Jerusalem.
327. She predicted the victory of Barak over the Canaanites.

328. He predicted the punishment that would befall David for undertaking a census of the people.

329. He criticized those who worshiped outwardly while not living holy lives.

330. This prophet predicted the prosperous reign of King Josiah.

331. He prophesied a blessing upon Jerusalem and the coming Day of the Lord.

332. He promised that a day of God's blessing would follow repentance.

333. He predicted captivity and disaster, but tempered it with the promise of the restoration of Jerusalem.

334. This prophet rebelled and ran from his assignment to preach to the citizens of Nineveh.

335. This woman of prayer saw the coming of the Messiah.

Which prophet said each of the following?

336. "I was no prophet, neither was I a prophet's son; but I was an herdman, and a gatherer of sycomore fruit: And the Lord took me as I followed the flock, and the Lord said unto me, Go, prophesy unto my people Israel."

337. "Then said the Lord unto me, Go yet, love a woman beloved of her friend, yet an adulteress,

according to the love of the Lord toward the children of Israel, who look to other gods, and love flagons of wine."

338. "Hold thy peace at the presence of the Lord God: for the day of the Lord is at hand: for the Lord hath prepared a sacrifice, he hath bid his guests."

339. "O Lord, how long shall I cry, and thou wilt not hear! even cry out unto thee of violence, and thou wilt not save!"

340. "The gates of the rivers shall be opened, and the palace shall be dissolved."

341. "Jeroboam shall die by the sword, and Israel shall surely be led away captive out of their own land."

342. "For thus saith the Lord of hosts, the God of Israel: The daughter of Babylon is like a threshingfloor, it is time to thresh her: yet a little while, and the time of her harvest shall come."

343. "And they shall beat their swords into plowshares, and their spears into pruninghooks: nation shall not lift up sword against nation, neither shall they learn war any more."

344. "God has numbered thy kingdom, and finished it. Thou art weighed in the balances, and art found wanting. Thy kingdom is divided, and given to the Medes and Persians."

345. "And I looked, and, behold, a whirlwind came out of the north, a great cloud, and a fire infolding itself, and a brightness was about it, and out of the midst thereof was the color of amber, out of the midst of the fire."

346. "Ye have sown much, and bring in little; ye eat, but ye have not enough; ye drink, but ye are not filled with drink; ye clothe you, but there is none warm; and he that earneth wages earneth wages to put it into a bag with holes."

347. "For the day of the Lord is near upon all the heathen: as thou hast done, it shall be done unto thee: thy reward shall return upon thine own head."

348. "In that day will I raise up the tabernacle of David that is fallen, and close up the breaches thereof; and I will raise up his ruins, and I will build it as in the days of old."

349. "I cried by reason of mine affliction unto the Lord, and he heard me; out of the belly of hell cried I, and thou heardest my voice."

350. "And he will stretch out his hand against the north, and destroy Assyria; and will make Nineveh a desolation, and dry like a wilderness."

CHAPTER 3

Living in Bible Times

The Bible gives us a very clear picture of what daily life was like long ago. See if you can answer these questions about living in Bible times.

Ritual and Worship

351. They were a group of powerful religious and political leaders during Jesus' time.

352. What items were contained in the ark of the covenant?

353. When was the first Sabbath observed?

354. This small but influential Jewish sect opposed the Pharisees.

355. The Ten Commandments, given to Moses on Mount Sinai, are a complete summary of moral law. Where in the Bible are they found?

356. Also called the Feast of Unleavened Bread, this holiday celebrates a time when the angel of

BIBLE BRAIN BUSTER

How much do you know about these religious practices in the Bible?

1. The word "sabbath" comes from a Hebrew word "shabath," meaning what?
2. What was used to anoint the priests of Israel?
3. According to Hebrew law, when does the Sabbath begin and end?
4. In the Old Testament, what word means "anointed"?
5. What instrument was used to call the faithful to prayer on the Sabbath?
6. How is the Sabbath supposed to be spent?
7. What New Testament word means "anointed"?
8. What does scripture prohibit on the Sabbath?
9. In the New Testament, what does the word "church" refer to?
10. What is another word for God's covenant with his people?

Answers: 1. To rest. 2. Olive oil. 3. From sundown on Friday until sundown on Saturday. 4. Messiah. 5. A trumpet. 6. In prayer and worship. 7. Christ. 8. Work. 9. A community of believers. 10. Testament

destruction killed the firstborn of Egypt, but spared the Israelite families.

357. On the Sabbath and at other times, it was the place where Jews met for prayer, as well as for instruction on the law of God.

358. It was during this Jewish festival celebrating thanksgiving for the harvest, also called the Feast of Weeks, that the Holy Spirit poured down upon the early Christians.

359. To offer up to God one's life or the life of an animal is called a _____.

360. This was the portable meeting place, or tent, where the Israelites worshiped God. The term also was used to refer to the temple.

361. God made several covenants, or agreements, with his creations. What was God's symbol of his covenant with Noah that humankind, the animals, and the earth would never again be destroyed by a flood?

362. According to Paul, all believers in Christ were anointed with this.

363. He built the first gold-covered altar.

364. According to the prophet Ezekiel, priests should not marry this type of woman.

365. In Israel, what was the punishment for disobeying a priest?

366. King Manasseh of Judah built altars for the worship of _____ and _____.

367. In the New Jerusalem, what takes the place of the temple?

368. There were twelve stones on the breastplate of the high priest. What was engraved upon these stones?

369. Who is the high priest of Israel now?

370. What were Urim and Thummin, two stones placed on the high priest's breastplate, used for?

371. God made this ceremonial rite mandatory for all descendants of Abraham as a sign of his covenant.

372. When the Israelites did these things, they broke the covenant made on Mount Sinai between God and Israel.

373. What five men were called to be the first priests of Israel?

374. What is the symbol of God's new covenant, instituted by Jesus?

BIBLE BRAIN BUSTER

Match the names of these common items from Bible times with their modern-day definition.

1. Sackbut
2. Alliyah
3. Krater
4. Kethon
5. Simlah

a. A large bowl or pot
b. A hooded, sheet-like garment
c. The guestroom area of a house
d. A musical instrument
e. A tunic made of animal skin

Answers: 1. d, 2. c, 3. a, 4. e, 5. b

375. This rite, used by the Jews to initiate devotees, also became a symbol of belief in Jesus.

Home Sweet Home

376. Where did the Israelites make their homes after being defeated by the Midianites?
377. What part of a house was torn up so that an afflicted man could get in to see Jesus?
378. On what part of the house did Samuel and Saul speak together after coming back into the city?
379. What daily needs did Jesus tell his followers not to worry about?
380. How was Elisha's room furnished?
381. What structure did Abraham call home?
382. This household item was also a symbol of life and family prestige among the Jews.
383. Who fell asleep—and then fell out of a window—while Paul was preaching?
384. The Jews built these on their roofs or in their courtyards in observance of the Feast of Tabernacles.
385. Where were the guest quarters in which the Last Supper took place?
386. When Mary traveled to a city in Judah to visit her cousin, whose house did she enter there?

387. When Jesus visited this home, one sister sat at his feet while the other busied herself with housework.

388. This man, who once piloted a giant boat, lived in a tent.

389. Who commanded that his descendants always live in tents?

390. Unfortunately, sometimes these creatures were found inside homes.

Daily Chores

391. What was used for cleaning in Jeremiah's time?

392. What skill did the Israelite women use to create gifts for the tabernacle?

393. Which king described "a virtuous woman" as "working willingly with her hands, bringing her food from afar, and rising while it is yet night"?

394. Jesus used this sewing tool as an example to explain how hard it would be for a rich man to enter heaven.

395. In one of Jesus' parables, what precious substance did some bridesmaids run out of because they hadn't brought any extra, while they waited for the bridegroom to come?

BIBLE BRAIN BUSTER

Jewish dietary law was very strict. Which of the following foods could be eaten and which were forbidden?

1. Fish with scales and fins
2. Meat that had been used in idol worship
3. Animals that have divided hoofs and chew their cud
4. Lizards
5. Scavenger birds
6. Pork
7. Insects
8. Meat from which the blood had been drained before cooking

Answers: 1. Allowed, 2. Forbidden, 3. Allowed, 4. Forbidden, 5. Forbidden, 6. Forbidden, 7. Allowed, 8. Allowed

Pastimes and Play

396. What prophet referred to children playing in the streets?
397. This enjoyable pastime was an important part of praise and worship.
398. What game of chance was employed immediately after the crucifixion?
399. In the Bible, dancing was often accompanied by this instrument.

BIBLE BRAIN BUSTER

Which of these statements are true and which are false?

1. Locusts, crickets, and grasshoppers were eaten as snacks and as meals in Bible times.
2. Jewish law required a barrier to be built around the roof on all houses to prevent falls during sleeping, socializing, working, or worship.
3. Formal schooling for both boys and girls began at age six.
4. In the time of Ruth, a land deal was sometimes sealed by the seller removing his shoe and presenting it to the buyer.
5. In both Old and New Testament times, there was a strict line between religious law and civil law.
6. Before he sent them away from the Garden of Eden, God made clothes for Adam and Eve from the feathers of fallen angels' wings.

---

400. Who said that people had to be like "little children" if they wanted to enter the kingdom of heaven?

Burial and Mourning

401. This rich man gave his tomb, which was hewn into a rock, as a burial place for Jesus.

BIBLE BRAIN BUSTER

True or false? (continued)

7. In New Testament times, a woman was required to give a coin offering at the temple when she gave birth to her first son.
8. Rainwater collected on the roof in a family's cistern was considered fit to drink.
9. Lamps were carefully extinguished at bedtime in Bible times.
10. A man paid a woman's father a fee called a mohar to marry her.

Answers: 1. True, 2. True, 3. False (Boys began school at six, girls received no formal education.), 4. True, 5. False (There was no separation between the two.), 6. False (God made their clothing from animal skins.), 7. True (Done in remembrance that the Egyptians lost their first-born sons when the Israelites gained their freedom.), 8. False (It contained impurities and was not considered safe to drink.), 9. False (Lamps were left burning all night to discourage thieves.), 10. True

402. Which prophet did God instruct not to mourn or weep for his dead wife?

403. How long was the usual mourning period among the Hebrews?

404. How long did the Israelites mourn Aaron's death?

405. Who asked a king's permission to return his father's body to Canaan?

406. Whose bodies, according to Revelation, will lie in the streets for three-and-a-half days without burial?

407. How long had Lazarus been in the tomb when Jesus arrived?

408. Which bereaved father was forbidden to mourn after his sons died in a fire?

409. What was used to seal the tomb in which Jesus was laid?

410. Jesus said, "Blessed are they that mourn, for _____."

411. Who shaved his head, tore his clothing, and fell to the ground when he heard that his children had died?

412. Who did the Lord send "to comfort all that mourn"?

413. What did a woman do that angered the disciples, but which Jesus said she had done in preparation for his burial?

414. Who had a pillar placed upon her grave after she died in childbirth?

415. After her husband and two sons died, this woman changed her name to "Mara" to show the bitterness of her life.

Bible Occupations

What jobs did these people hold?

416. Shadrach, Meshach, and Abednego
417. Zipporah
418. Julius
419. Gehazi
420. Baruch
421. Zacchaeus
422. Priscilla and Aquila
423. Lydia
424. Gideon
425. Simon and Andrew

The Golden Years

People were known to live to a very ripe old age in Bible times. Adam lived to be 930! Can you name these biblical seniors?

426. This leader still had his eyesight and his strength when he died at age 120.
427. Hale and hearty at age 85, he asked for the mountain that had been promised to him.
428. At age 147, this man implored his son to take him out of Egypt and bury him "with my fathers."

429. He was the longest-lived man ever when he died: 969 years old.

430. An angel told this married couple that they were going to have a baby—even though both were quite old.

431. This son of Noah fathered Arphaxad at age 100, two years after the flood; then lived another 500 years and fathered more children.

BIBLE BRAIN BUSTER

Which of the following articles of clothing or adornment were worn by women, by men—or by both—in Bible times?

1. Girdle
2. Earrings
3. Sandals
4. Purse

5. Mourning apparel
6. Phylacteries
7. Veil
8. Headdress

Answers: 1. Both (used to secure outer garments), 2. Women, 3. Both, 4. Men, 5. Both, 6. Men (contained scrolls inscribed with the Law), 7. Women, 8. Both

432. In his later years this king couldn't get warm, even when he was bundled in clothing.

433. He was 600 years old when the earth was destroyed by floodwaters.

434. God changed this patriarch's name when he was 99 years old.

435. This king had foot problems in his old age.

Buildings and Other Structures

436. What did the people of Jerusalem do on their rooftops that caused Jeremiah to prophesy their downfall?

437. This king of Israel built the capital city at Samaria.

438. He was "the father of such that dwell in tents."

439. According to Jesus, what building would be so thoroughly destroyed that not one stone would remain standing upon another?

440. The Egyptian treasure cities of Raamses and Pithom were built by these people.

441. They plundered the Syrians' tents after the soldiers had fled the camp.

442. Whose children perished when the house in which they were feasting collapsed in a storm?

443. Whose palace had marble pillars and beds made of silver and gold?

444. He rebuilt Jericho during the reign of Ahab.

445. In John's vision, how many gates are there in the walls of the city of New Jerusalem?

446. What were the gates of New Jerusalem made of, according to John's vision?

447. Who built the city of Enoch to the east of Eden?

448. This king of Tyre sent materials and workers to build David a house.

449. Who built the ancient city of Babylon?

450. In whose tent was Goliath's armor stored?

451. God gave the specifications for building what tent?

452. Paul escaped through a window in the wall of what city?

453. This son of Jacob nearly lost his life at the bottom of a cistern.

454. What door on earth did God shut?

455. Jonadab commanded that his descendants always make their homes in what structure?

Clothing in Ancient Times

456. Clothing of this color was highly prized.

457. Jeremiah and Ezekiel criticized women who wore this.

458. What was John the Baptist's tunic made of?

459. Jacob is the only person mentioned in the Bible who wore this article of clothing.

460. Captives were humiliated by their enemies by being forced to wear this.

BIBLE BRAIN BUSTER

If there had been supermarket tabloids in ancient times, the following biblical murders may have inspired sensational headlines in the checkout aisle. Match the "headline" to its Old Testament "news story" by naming the victim.

1. Moses slays man, seeks refuge in Midian
2. Grandma Athaliah goes on royal killing spree in wake of son's death
3. "Milk killer" Jael "nails" sleeping victim
4. Zimri kills drunken king, steals throne
5. Ehud uses left hand to bury knife in royal victim's "spare tire"
6. Hazael real "wet blanket," takes king's life and throne
7. Brothers Rechab and Baanah kill, behead sleeping victim in vengeance killing
8. Evil king slain by top captain Pekah

a. Ben-hadad
b. Eglon, King of Moab
c. Ishbosheth
d. Pekahiah
e. Her grandchildren
f. Sisera
g. A cruel Egyptian
h. Elah

Answers: 1. g (Exodus 2:11–15), 2. e (2 Kings 11:1), 3. f (Judges 4:18–22), 4. b (1 Kings 16:9–10), 5. b (Judges 3:15–23), 6. a (2 Kings 8:9–15), 7. c (2 Samuel 4:5–8), 8. d (2 Kings 15:23–25)

49

461. To take off this item of clothing was considered an act of reverence and respect.

462. Worn by Hebrew women on special occasions, it covered the face.

463. This fabric was much-used in Bible times, and the best quality could be found in Egypt.

464. Joseph was given this very special article of clothing as boy.

465. The Israelites did this to the hems of their garments to remind them to keep the Lord's commandments.

Money Earned, Money Spent

Where in the Bible do the following references to money appear?

466. "I will give thee money for the field; take it of me, and I will bury my dead there."

467. ". . . And commanded them that they should take nothing for their journey, save a staff only; no scrip, no bread, no money in the purse."

468. ". . . She sent and called for the lords of the Philistines, saying, 'Come up this once, for he hath shewed me all his heart.' Then the lords of the Philistines came up unto her, and brought money in their hand."

469. "And Moses gave the money of them that were redeemed unto Aaron and to his sons, according to the word of the Lord, as the Lord commanded Moses."

470. "And when they were come to Capernaum, they that received tribute money came to Peter, and said, Doth not your master pay tribute?"

471. "The heads thereof judge for reward, and the priests thereof teach for hire, and the prophets thereof divine for money: yet will they lean upon the Lord, and say, Is not the Lord among us? none evil can come upon us."

472. ". . . When he saw that he was condemned, repented himself, and brought again the thirty pieces of silver to the chief priests and elders."

473. "He drove them all out of the temple, and the sheep, and the oxen; and poured out the changers' money, and overthrew the tables."

474. "We have drunken our water for money; our wood is sold unto us."

475. "And Menahem exacted the money of Israel, even of all the mighty men of wealth, of each man fifty shekels of silver, to give to the king of Assyria."

476. "For the love of money is the root of all evil."

477. "And unto one he gave five talents, to another two, and to another one; to every man according to his several ability."

478. "Thou shalt not give him thy money upon usury, nor lend him thy victuals for increase."
479. "I was afraid, and went and hid thy talent in the earth."
480. "When money failed in the land of Egypt, and in the land of Canaan, all the Egyptians came unto Joseph, and said, Give us bread: for why should we die in thy presence?"

Food and Drink

481. Esau sold his birthright for a meal. What did he eat?
482. Abraham fed these foods to heavenly visitors.
483. Jesus made a meal out of this for five thousand people.
484. What sweet food did Samson find in a lion's carcass?
485. What food did Jesus eat after the Resurrection to prove that he wasn't a ghost?
486. What beverage was traditionally offered to guests to show hospitality and good cheer?
487. What fruits did the Israelites bring out of the land of Canaan?
488. Gideon offered these foods to an angel, but the angel did not eat them.
489. The Israelites longed for these familiar foods while in the wilderness.

BIBLE BRAIN BUSTER

Fill in the blanks to name these common household items in Bible times.

1. For the tabernacle, Bezaleel "made the vessels which were upon the table, his dishes, and his _____, and his bowls, and his covers to cover withal, of pure gold."
2. The children of Israel gathered manna, ground it, "and baked it in _____, and made cakes of it: and the taste of it was as the taste of fresh oil."
3. Gideon "rose up early on the morrow, and thrust fleece together, and wringed the dew out of the fleece, a _____ full of water."
4. After Jesus fed the five thousand, the disciples, "took up of the fragments that remained twelve _____ full."
5. Elisha told his servant, "Set on the great _____, and seethe pottage for the sons of the prophets."
6. Jesus said, ". . . Ye make clean the outside of the _____ and of the _____, but within they are full of extortion and excess."
7. When they left Egypt, the Israelites "took their dough before it was leavened, their _____ being bound up in their clothes upon their shoulders."
8. Jesus "poureth water into a _____, and began to wash the disciples' feet."

Answers: 1. Spoons (Exodus 37:16), 2. Pans (Numbers 11:8), 3. Bowl (Judges 6:38), 4. Baskets (Matthew 14:20), 5. Pot (2 Kings 4:38), 6. Cup, platter (Matthew 25), 7. Kneadingtroughs (Exodus 2:34), 8. Basin (John 13:5)

490. The Lord provided this miraculous "bread from heaven" for the Israelites every day for forty years.

Flavorings, Spices, and Herbs

491. This was used not only as a seasoning, but in sacrifices made to God.
492. Which prophet ate a book and found the taste sweet?
493. Jesus called this spice the least of all seeds, but when it is grown, the greatest among herbs.
494. This man also ate a sweet book—only to have the taste turn bitter afterwards.
495. What kind of herbs did the Israelites eat with the Passover meal?
496. This kind of bread tastes sweet to man, but afterwards "his mouth shall be filled with gravel."
497. Jesus said that after the Resurrection, his followers would be able to drink this.
498. This substance sweetened John the Baptist's diet of locusts.
499. This sour wine was offered to Jesus before his death.
500. Moses made the bitter waters of Marah drinkable by doing this.

Love, Marriage, and Family

501. The Bible compares God's love for his people to what earthly relationship?

502. According to Proverbs, what is a father's duty?

503. Where did the first marriage take place?

504. Who gave the marriage of Adam and Eve as a model for all men and women?

505. A father was supposed to encourage his family in what area?

506. Jesus called this kind of love "the first and great commandment."

507. Where was the first wedding Jesus attended held?

508. Jesus said, "Greater love hath no man than this, _____."

509. How should a person go about loving his neighbor?

510. Who said, "Marriage is honorable in all"?

Crime and Punishment

511. He stole eleven hundred shekels of silver from his mother, but he returned it.

512. He swindled Jacob in a marriage bargain.

513. Who did Jesus say would speak in court on behalf of his followers?

514. Pharaoh burned down this city of Israel.

515. When the Assyrians deported the Israelites, how many of the twelve tribes of Israel were left?

516. He murdered Shallum and took over the throne of Israel.

517. This robber was released from prison on Passover.

518. He was imprisoned after being wrongly accused of trying to seduce Potiphar's wife.

519. Even after an earthquake opened the prison doors, these two men chose to remain in jail.

520. Who was in exile in Gesher for three years after ordering the killing of his brother, Amnon?

521. Who were the first people in the Bible to be punished by exile?

522. This Assyrian king carried the Israelites into exile.

523. What happened to Paul and Silas after they had cast a demon out of a fortune-teller?

524. According to the laws of Moses, how many witnesses were required for a man to be tried and put to death?

525. He was imprisoned by the Philistines.

526. This apostle was exiled to the island of Patmos.

527. This reptile lied to a woman.

528. Who bribed those guarding Jesus' tomb to say that the disciples had stolen his body?

529. According to the Law, what is the punishment for adultery?

530. Which king of Israel was put in jail for defying Assyrian authority?

531. How many false witnesses appeared before the council to testify against Jesus at his trial?

532. Who was the first murderer described in the Bible?

533. After hearing his defense, these three rulers decided that Paul did not deserve to be punished.

534. They were banished to the desert by Abraham.

535. Which prophet's son was not above taking bribes?

536. Which one of Moses' relatives suggested that he appoint judges to help him handle all the cases brought before him?

537. Who was exiled to Nod after committing murder?

538. This king of Babylon burned down Jerusalem.

539. Which blind king died in exile in Babylon?

540. Which prophet was exiled to Egypt along with the people of Judah?

541. Where did Cain murder Abel?

542. Who bribed Delilah to find out the secret of Samson's great strength?

543. Which disciple was a thief?

544. How long were the Israelites in exile in Egypt?

545. He burned Joab's field of barley just to get his attention.

546. Who was imprisoned for criticizing King Herod's marriage to Herodias?

547. After killing an Egyptian to save a fellow Hebrew, this man fled to Midian.

548. This son of David led a revolt against his own father.

549. She stole idols from her father.

550. Who killed Joab on instructions from Solomon?

551. Why didn't the priests and rulers choose to punish Peter and John at their trial?

552. Who reigned as king of Israel after killing the kings of Israel and Judah, and having Jezebel murdered?

553. Who burned David's city of Ziklag?

554. Who falsely accused his own brothers of being spies and had them put in prison?

555. Who burned down the tower of Schechem, killing a thousand men and women?

556. Which seer was imprisoned for prophesying doom for King Asa?

557. He murdered Pekah and took over the throne of Israel.

558. Which king of Judah was imprisoned and blinded for defying Babylonian authority?

559. David committed adultery with this beautiful woman.

560. Which two apostles were jailed in Jerusalem for preaching the gospel?

CHAPTER 4

Bible Geography

Barren deserts, lush farmlands, mountains, and seas—these and more are to be found in the lands of the Bible. Find out how much you know about Bible terrain.

Mountainous Country

In the Bible, the words "hill" and "mountain" are often used to mean land of the same elevation. For instance, the "mountain of Judah" referred to in the book of Joshua appears as "hill country" in the gospel of Luke. Can you name the following hills—or mountains—of biblical proportions?

561. Where did God tell Abraham to take his son Isaac to be sacrificed?
562. Deborah and Barak came down this mountain to defeat Sisera.
563. The Philistines killed Saul and Jonathan here.

564. What is Moses' burial place?
565. On what mountain did Elijah challenge the priests of Baal?
566. Where did Jesus weep over the city of Jerusalem?
567. Where did Moses bring forth water from the rock?
568. Moses spoke with God on this mountain.
569. Where did the ark run aground?
570. From what mountain did Moses view the promised land?

BIBLE BRAIN BUSTER

Each of the following is either a mountain, a river, a sea, an island, or a city in the Bible. Do you know which is which?

1. Nebo
2. Horeb
3. Pison
4. Melita
5. Ararat
6. Tarsus
7. Arimathea
8. Succoth
9. Gihon
10. Patmos
11. Ebal
12. Shushan
13. Hiddekel
14. Gomorrah
15. Gilead

Answers: 1. Mountain, 2. Mountain, 3. River, 4. Island, 5. Mountain, 6. City, 7. City, 8. City, 9. River, 10. Island, 11. Mountain, 12. City, 13. River, 14. City, 15. City

BIBLE BRAIN BUSTER

Which of these statements are true and which are false?

1. The New Testament word "gehenna," meaning "hell," comes from the Hebrew "ge'hinnom," (Hinnon Valley) in Jerusalem, where the residents burned their garbage.
2. The Dead Sea is so salty that a person would sink in it like a stone.
3. In Bible times, caves were used as homes, storage places, tombs, and hiding places.
4. The good Samaritan didn't really go "down" from Jerusalem to Jericho, but east.
5. A person riding a fast camel across the desert could travel up to seventy miles in one day.
6. Jericho is the world's oldest city.

Answers: 1. True, 2. False (A person would float like a cork.), 3. True, 4. False (He went down and east: Jericho is 3,300 feet lower than Jerusalem, and fifteen miles to the east.), 5. True, 6. True (It was first occupied in 9000 B.C.)

Cities and Fortresses

571. This square city had walls made of jasper.
572. Where was Saul proclaimed king?
573. What city did Peter, Andrew, and Philip call home?
574. At Joppa, Jonah boarded a ship bound for what city?

BIBLE BRAIN BUSTER

Match each of these rivers to the land associated with it.

1. Tigris
2. Nile
3. Kishon
4. Ahava
5. Pharpar
6. Jordan

a. Babylonia
b. Megiddo
c. Damascas
d. Egypt
e. Palestine
f. Eden

Answers: 1. f, 2. d, 3. b, 4. a, 5. c, 6. e

575. Solomon built these city walls.

576. Elisha visited an ailing king in this city.

577. It was here that Jesus raised a widow's son from the dead.

578. Of all the seven cities of Asia, this one is most highly praised.

579. Where was the tabernacle after the Israelites defeated the Canaanites?

580. King Josiah died here.

581. Timothy and Silas stayed here while Paul traveled to Athens.

582. The walls of this city fell flat at the sound of trumpets.

583. Gideon punished the people of this city for refusing food to his hungry soldiers.

584. King Nebuchadnezzar ruled this city.
585. Paul hailed from this city.
586. What was Goliath's hometown?
587. Zacchaeus the tax collector lived in this city.
588. This is where Jesus' followers were first called Christians.
589. In what Philistine city did the inhabitants worship Baal-zebub?
590. Nebuchadnezzar tore down the walls of this city.

Bodies of Water

591. Pharaoh's men drowned in this body of water.
592. Where did Jesus walk upon the waters?
593. Ezra proclaimed a fast at this river.
594. Where did a river turn to blood?
595. Naaman washed in this river to be cured of leprosy.
596. What is the Dead Sea called in the Bible?
597. Elijah lived by this body of water.
598. After the Resurrection, Jesus appeared to his disciples at this body of water.
599. The river in the Garden of Eden split into these four rivers.
600. In what river did John baptize those who had repented of their sins?

BIBLE BRAIN BUSTER

In Bible times, water was fetched from a well and brought home in jars. Unscramble the locations of these "well-known" wells.

1. TLEEMHEHB
2. BREABHESE
3. ANARH
4. ARAMISA
5. RAGER
6. RANHO
7. DEKSAH
8. HARMA
9. AIDNIM

Answers: 1. Bethlehem, 2. Beersheba, 3. Haran, 4. Samaria, 5. Gerar, 6. Nahor, 7. Kadesh, 8. Ramah, 9. Midian

Deserts and Plains

In the Bible, a desert was more than just a dry, barren area. It could be an uncultivated place, or one where animals grazed. Name the book of the Bible where each of these verses about deserts or plains appears. For extra credit, cite chapter and verse!

601. "Let us go, we pray thee, three days' journey into the desert, and sacrifice unto the Lord our God."

602. "Thou shalt come to the plain of Tabor, and there shall meet thee three men going up to

God to Beth-el, one carrying three kids, and another carrying three loaves of bread, and another carrying a bottle of wine."

603. "He departed thence by ship into a desert place apart: and when the people had heard thereof, they followed him on foot out of the cities."

604. "And Abram passed through the land unto the place of Sichem, unto the plain of Moreh."

605. "And the child grew, and waxed strong in spirit, and was in the deserts till the day of his shewing unto Israel."

Islands and Oases

The following verses refer to islands—land in the middle of water—and oases, those life-saving water holes in the middle of barren land. Again, name the book of the Bible where they appear; chapter and verse if you can!

606. "I John, who also am your brother, and companion in tribulation, and in the kingdom and patience of Jesus Christ, was in the isle that is called Patmos, for the word of God, and for the testimony of Jesus Christ."

607. "For the Lord shall comfort Zion: he will

comfort all her waste places; and he will make her wilderness like Eden, and her desert like the garden of the Lord."

608. "And Moses lifted up his hand, and with his rod he smote the rock twice: and the water came out abundantly, and the congregation drank, and their beasts also."

609. "And when they were escaped, then they knew that the island was called Melita. And the barbarous people shewed us no little kindness: for they kindled a fire, and received us every one."

610. ". . . For in the wilderness shall waters break out, and streams in the desert. And the parched ground shall become a pool, and the thirsty land springs of water."

Valleys

Each of the following occurred in a valley. Do you know which one was the setting for each of these events?

611. King Josiah was killed in battle.

612. Goliath was slain by David.

613. Jehoshaphat and his people blessed the Lord.

614. All the nations were gathered.

615. Ahaz sacrificed his children to Baalim.

BIBLE BRAIN BUSTER

Geography has a lot to do with climate
and weather conditions. Name the Bible person
or persons associated with these weather events.

1. He survived a great flood.
2. He suffered drought by day and frost by night.
3. They were in a prison shaken by an earthquake.
4. He was taken to heaven by a whirlwind.
5. He wrung dew from fleece.
6. He quieted the wind.
7. They died amid hailstones.
8. He brought thunder and hail upon Egypt with
   his rod.

*Answers: 1. Noah (Genesis 6–9), 2. Jacob (Genesis 31:40),
3. Paul and Silas (Acts 16:25–26), 4. Elijah (2 Kings 2:11),
5. Gideon (Judges 6:37), 6. Jesus (Matthew 14:32),
7. Amorites (Joshua 10:11), 8. Moses (Exodus 9:23)*

Biblical Travels

These people made some famous Bible journeys. Who
were they?

616. He brought his family to settle in Nazareth
     after an angel appeared to him in a dream.
617. Though he brought the Israelites to Canaan, he
     never entered that land himself.
618. He traveled from Bethel to Jericho with the
     prophet Elijah.

619. She followed her mother-in-law to Bethlehem.

620. They followed a star to Jerusalem.

621. These ten brothers traveled together to Egypt to buy grain.

622. This group of twelve men traveled without money, food, or a change of clothing.

623. The Lord sent him to preach to the people of Nineveh.

624. She traveled by camel to meet her future husband.

625. He went with Paul on his first missionary journey.

CHAPTER 5

The Natural World in Bible Times

Animals, plants, the minerals of the earth—even stars in the sky—all had important parts to play in the story of the Bible.

Fishes Great and Small

With many varieties of fish plentiful in the River Nile; the Sea of Galilee; and the Jordan, Kishon, and Jabbok Rivers; fish was a major source of food and fishing was a common occupation in Bible times.

626. How many of the disciples were fishermen, and what were their names?
627. According to Genesis, who had dominion over the fish of the sea?
628. How long was Jonah trapped in the belly of the great fish?

629. What happened to the river Nile when Moses smote the waters with his rod and caused all the fish to die?

630. Jesus promised to make them "fishers of men."

631. God blessed him, adding, "And the fear of you shall be . . . upon all the fishes of the sea."

632. Jesus told Peter to cast his line to catch a fish with something special in its mouth. What was in the fish's mouth?

633. "As the fishes that are taken in an evil net . . . so are the sons of men snared in _____."

634. Who wanted to know, ". . . what man is there of you, whom if his son . . . ask a fish, will he give him a serpent?"

635. What exceptionally wise man "spake . . . of beasts, and of fowl, and of creeping things, and of fishes"?

The Birds and the Beasts

636. Who had a donkey that could speak?

637. This youngster killed a lion and a bear to rescue one sheep.

638. What animal did the Lord send to feed the Israelites in the wilderness?

639. When Jesus went to Jerusalem at Passover, where did he find the sellers of doves, oxen, and sheep?

BIBLE BRAIN BUSTER

Fill in the blank to finish these Bible verses about birds.

1. "How often would I have gathered thy children together, as a _____ doth gather her brood under her wings."

2. "Every three years once came the ships of Tarshish bringing gold, and silver, ivory, and apes, and _____."

3. "The eye that mocketh at his father, and despiseth to obey his mother, the _____ of the valley shall pick it out."

4. "I bare you on _____'s wings, and brought you unto myself."

5. "My love; behold, thou art fair; thou hast _____'s eyes."

6. "He brought _____, and satisfied them with the bread of heaven."

7. "But these . . . ye shall not eat . . . the glede, and the _____, and the vulture after his kind. . . ."

8. "Doth the _____ fly by thy wisdom, and stretch her wings toward the south?"

9. "Before the _____ crow, thou shalt deny me thrice."

10. "There shall the great _____ make her nest, and lay, and hatch, and gather under her shadow."

Answers: 1. Hen (Luke 13:34), 2. Peacocks (2 Chronicles 9:21), 3. Ravens (Proverbs 30:17), 4. Eagles (Exodus 19:4), 5. Doves (Song of Solomon 1:15), 6. Quails (Psalms 106:40), 7. Kite (Leviticus 11:14), 8. Hawk (Job 39:26), 9. Cock (Matthew 26:75), 10. Owl (Isaiah 34:15)

640. Rebekah traveled to meet her future husband on one.

641. These animals were used to pull a plow.

642. He was the first mentioned in the Bible who kept sheep.

643. The Israelites cast a golden idol in the shape of this animal.

644. Who were sent out as "sheep in the midst of wolves," and told to be "wise as serpents, and harmless as doves"?

645. What animal brought Noah proof that the floodwaters had receded and it was safe to leave the ark?

BIBLE BRAIN BUSTER

Arrange the ten plagues in the order in which they occurred.

Gnats	Hailstones
Darkness	Death of firstborn
Lice	Egyptians
Flies	Boils
Locusts	Plague upon the cattle
River Nile turned	of Egypt
to blood	

Answers: 1. River Nile turned to blood 2. Frogs, 3. Gnats, 4. Flies, 5. Plague upon the cattle of Egypt, 6. Boils, 7. Hailstones, 8. Locusts, 9. Darkness, 10. Death of firstborn Egyptians

646. The call of this animal marked Peter's denial of Jesus.
647. The blood of this animal saved the firstborn children of the Israelites from harm.
648. Jesus entered Jerusalem riding on this animal's back.
649. Who sent three hundred foxes, armed with fire, to destroy the Philistines' cornfields, vineyards, and olive trees?
650. Who had a pet ewe lamb that he fed from the table and raised as one of his own children?

Reptiles, Insects, and Amphibians

651. God sent ten plagues upon Egypt to convince Pharaoh to let the Hebrew people go free. What was the eighth plague?
652. This reptile tricked Eve into disobeying God.
653. What four things on earth are small, but very wise?
654. Along with the ferret, chameleon, snail, and mole, this reptile was considered unclean by Mosaic Law.
655. What insect was the fourth of God's plagues visited upon Egypt?
656. Who lived on a diet of bitter-tasting locusts sweetened with wild honey?

657. While on the island of Melita, Paul was bitten by this poisonous reptile, but did not die.

658. They created a sweet surprise inside the carcass of a lion.

659. In John's vision, these insects came out of the smoke of the pit.

660. In the second plague, Egypt's borders were besieged by these creatures.

All That Glitters

Precious and semiprecious stones, precious metals, and all types of jewelry appear in the pages of the Bible. Answer these questions correctly, and you will shine!

661. How many gemstones are set in the breastplate of the high priest?

662. According to Proverbs, these can be considered a precious jewel.

663. What article of jewelry did the descendants of Ishmael wear?

664. Jesus said that the search for the kingdom of heaven was like a merchant seeking this gemstone.

665. Why did the Israelites give up their jewels?

666. This semiprecious stone was used in the construction of the temple.

BIBLE BRAIN BUSTER

Unscramble these words to find the twelve stones set into the high priest's breastplate.

1. ZOPAT
2. REDELAM
3. NIDDOMA
4. GEATA
5. RELYB
6. SEPARJ
7. NOXY
8. MYTAEHTS
9. URASIDS
10. RUCCBLAEN
11. HEASPRIP
12. EGRILU

Answers: 1. Topaz, 2. Emerald, 3. Diamond, 4. Agate, 5. Beryl, 6. Jasper, 7. Onyx, 8. Amethyst, 9. Sardius, 10. Carbuncle, 11. Sapphire, 12. Ligure

667. Who promised to lay foundations of sapphires and to make windows of agates and gates of carbuncles?

668. In John's vision, what was surrounded by a rainbow "like unto an emerald"?

669. The price of wisdom is compared to the cost of these precious stones.

670. Abraham's servant gave these items of jewelry to Rebekah at the well.

671. Who will be God's jewels?

672. What man received a ring from his father upon his return home?

BIBLE BRAIN BUSTER

**The "burning" question: What fiery object
is associated with each of these Bible people?**

1. Samson's bindings made of _____ became as
   burned by fire.
2. _____ of fire sat upon the apostles.
3. Amaziah burned _____.
4. Shadrach, Meshach, and Abednego were thrown
   into the fiery _____.
5. The ten virgins brought their _____.
6. Isaiah's lips were touched by a live _____.
7. Moses harkened unto the burning _____.
8. God looked through the _____ of fire.

*Answers: 1. Flax (Judges 15:14), 2. Tongues (Acts 2:3),
3. Incense (2 Chronicles 25:14), 4. Furnace (Daniel 3:20),
5. Lamps (Matthew 25:2), 6. Coal (Isaiah 6:6–7), 7. Bush
(Exodus 3:2), 8. Pillar (Exodus 14:24)*

673. In Proverbs, "As an _____ of gold . . . so is a
     wise reprover upon an obedient ear."
674. Whose men found so many precious jewels and
     riches on the bodies of a conquered army that it
     took them three days to gather it all?
675. This ruler gave Joseph a ring from his own
     hand in return for interpreting a dream.

Sun, Moon, and Stars

676. Who described himself as the "bright and morning star"?

677. What celestial body did God create when he made "the lesser light"?

678. When God appeared to Abram (Abraham) in a vision, what did he say would be like the number of stars in heaven?

679. Who said, "Canst thou bind the sweet influences of Pleiades, or loose the bands of Orion? Canst thou bring forth Mazzaroth in his season? or canst thou guide Arcturus with his sons? Knowest thou the ordinances of heaven? Canst thou set the dominion thereof in the earth?"

680. What did Ezekiel observe twenty-five men doing in the temple that caused God to be angry?

681. King Nebuchadnezzar called upon these stargazers to interpret his dreams, but they failed.

682. Who "telleth the number of the stars" and "calleth them all by their names"?

683. King Josiah commanded that all the vessels from the temple used for this activity be burned.

684. What heavenly sign announced the birth of Jesus?

685. God created lights in the sky for what reasons?

Fire and Ice

686. Upon what two sinful cities did the Lord rain brimstone and fire?

687. What form did the Lord take while helping Moses lead the Israelites out of Egypt?

688. This man's friends turned away from him, as cold as ice and snow.

689. According to Proverbs, "As snow in summer, and as rain in harvest, so _____."

690. This gift from heaven was like crystals of frost on the ground.

691. In John's vision, who had feet like pillars of fire?

692. Inhabitants of Melita did this for Paul because of the rain and cold.

693. Who wrote, "For the sun is no sooner risen with a burning heat, but it withereth the grass, and the flower thereof falleth . . . so also shall the rich man fade away in his ways."

694. Who is like a branch that has been cast into a fire and burned?

695. After Noah did this God was pleased; and promised that the cycles of seedtime and harvest, cold and heat, summer and winter, day and night, would never cease.

The Bible "Rainbow"

696. Lydia, a Philippian, sold cloth of this color.
697. In what color were the Assyrians, neighbors of Aholah and Aholibah, clothed?
698. What would greenish and reddish hues on one's garment signify?
699. In John's vision, what color was the horse that appeared when the first seal was opened?
700. "He maketh me to lie down in _____ pastures."
701. Moses brought Israel from this colorfully named body of water.
702. In Deborah's song, who rode on white asses?
703. The Roman soldiers clothed Jesus in this color, placed a crown of thorns on his head, and mocked him.
704. Hosea likened himself to this green object.
705. A horse of this color appeared when the third seal was opened.
706. Mordecai's "royal apparel" contained what regal colors?
707. Joseph's brothers would not speak civilly to him because of this garment.
708. In John's vision, what was the rider of the black horse carrying?

BIBLE BRAIN BUSTER

Match the animal to its rather unpleasant Bible role.

1. Jesus cast a legion of unclean spirits out of a man and into their midst.
2. The Israelites were bitten by these during their sojourn in the wilderness.
3. In Revelation, they were tails for the horses.
4. They ate the body of Jezebel.
5. It destroyed the plant that had shaded Jonah.
6. It bit Paul on the hand.
7. They appeared to the prophet Joel in a vision.
8. It cured snakebite.
9. Jesus said that a loveless father would give this to his child.

a. Dogs
b. Viper
c. Worm
d. Swine
e. Bronze snake on a pole
f. Fiery serpents
g. Scorpion
h. Locusts
i. Snakes

Answers: 1. d (Mark 5:13), 2. f (Numbers 21:6), 3. i (Revelation 9:19), 4. a (2 Kings 9:36), 5. c (Jonah 4:7), 6. b (Acts 28:3–6), 7. h (Joel 1:1–4), 8. e (Numbers 21:8–9), 9. g (Luke 11:12)

709. After Peter, James, and John saw Jesus' "face shine as the sun, and his raiment . . . white as the light," what happened next?

710. After the flood, what was the token of God's covenant with Noah?

Trees, Plants, and Crops

711. This plant was used to cleanse and purify.

712. Jesus was given a piece of this plant as a "scepter."

713. This place was known as the "city of palm trees."

714. Jonah was glad of the shade this plant provided for him—although it didn't last long.

715. What type of branch did the dove carry to Noah in its beak?

716. An apple tree appears only in this book of the Bible.

717. This bitter-tasting plant was used as a symbol of disaster and misery.

718. Used in one of Jesus' parables, this plant has the smallest of all seeds.

719. What famous boat was made of gopher wood?

720. Jesus spied this tree from a distance, but was angered to find no fruit on it.

721. In the parable of the sower, some of the seeds were killed by these.

722. On what day of creation did God make green plants?
723. Because they had not grown up, these grains were spared in the plague of hail upon Egypt.
724. The prophet Jeremiah saw a branch of this tree in a vision.
725. After a day's journey, Elijah sat and rested beneath this tree.

CHAPTER 6

Bible History and Epic

War, intrigue, romance, heroism, suspense, laughter, and sorrow—the Bible has all this and more.

In the Beginning

726. What moved across the waters when the earth was still empty and formless?
727. How did God prevent Adam and Eve from returning to the garden?
728. Who gave all the creatures of the earth their names?
729. What was the serpent's punishment for tricking Eve?
730. After he had created the world, how did God water all the plants on earth?
731. Adam and Eve were told not to eat fruit from what tree?
732. How did Adam become a living soul?

BIBLE BRAIN BUSTER

True or false?

1. "Easter" is mentioned nowhere in the Bible.
2. "Moses" means "drawn out" of the water.
3. Jesus never sang a song with his disciples.
4. Rebekah offered water to a man and his oxen.
5. Andrew was also known as Cephas.
6. Judas Iscariot died by hanging.
7. An angel of the Lord afflicted Herod with a fatal case of worms.
8. While Paul was preaching, a man went to sleep—and fell out a window.

Answers: 1. False (Acts 12:4), 2. True (Exodus 2:10), 3. False (Mark 14:26), 4. False (Genesis 24:19), 5. False (John 1:42), 6. True (Matthew 27:5), 7. True (Acts 12:20–23), 8. True (Acts 20:9)

733. What were Eve's and Adam's punishments for their disobedience?

734. Why did Adam call his companion "woman"?

735. What did Adam and Eve do when they heard God's voice in the garden?

736. What did God use to create Adam?

737. What did God make on the fourth day of creation?

738. In what direction did God put Eden?

739. What did God give Adam and Eve as their meat?

740. What divides the waters above from the waters below?

Biblical Battles

741. Who slaughtered 185,000 Assyrian soldiers?

742. Why did King Pekah of Israel kill 20,000 men of Judea in one day?

743. The Syrian soldiers were struck blind by this.

744. This country's army was defeated at the Red Sea.

745. What came from heaven to help Joshua and his army defeat the Amorites?

746. Who said, "Think not that I am come to send peace on earth: I came not to send peace, but a sword"?

747. How many Midianites did Gideon and his men kill in battle?

748. What Syrian king ran when the people of Israel killed 100,000 of his soldiers in one day?

749. King David's army slew 47,000 soldiers of what enemy army?

750. What Judaean king led an army that killed 500,000 Israelite soldiers?

751. In John's vision, who gathered the kings of the earth and others to the battle of the day of God?

752. How did Israel win the battle against the nation of Amalek?

753. What did Jehoshaphat do that made God destroy the armies of the Ammonites, Moabites, and Edomites?

754. Who fell, broke his neck, and died upon hearing that the Philistines had captured the ark of God?

755. Who slew 7,000 Syrians in chariots and another 40,000 on foot?

The Gospel of Jesus

756. Who told the shepherds about the birth of Jesus?

757. Why did Jesus tell Peter to catch a fish with a coin in its mouth?

758. What happened to Jesus' seamless coat after he was crucified?

759. This woman mistook the resurrected Jesus for a gardener.

760. What miracle did Jesus perform for the widow of Nain?

761. Who washed the disciples' feet?

762. How were the wise men warned not to return to Herod?

763. This ruler decreed that everyone must journey to their home city to be taxed.

764. Who warned Joseph to take his family and flee to Egypt?

BIBLE BRAIN BUSTER

Name the book of the Bible where these things or events can be found.

1. Jesus raises Lazarus.
2. The walls of Jericho fall.
3. Four horses of different colors appear.
4. God calls Moses.
5. Jesus gives the Sermon on the Mount.
6. Ravens feed Elijah.
7. Paul is shipwrecked.
8. A man is hung on the gallows he built.

Answers: 1. John, 2. Joshua, 3. Revelation, 4. Exodus, 5. Matthew, 6. 1 Kings, 7. Acts, 8. Esther

765. How did Judas betray Jesus?

766. Where was Jesus when a woman came and anointed him with precious ointment?

767. What did the disciples do as Jesus prayed in the garden at Gethsemane?

768. Who coaxed Jesus to perform the first miracle, at a wedding in Cana?

769. Who tried to walk to Jesus on the water, but became afraid and faltered?

770. Who prepared Jesus' body for burial and placed it in the sepulcher?

771. What did the chief priests do with the thirty pieces of silver that Judas returned to them?

BIBLE BRAIN BUSTER

Answer these questions about the temple built by Solomon.

1. The temple was built on this mountain.
2. What were the dimensions of the temple?
3. What was the worth of the gold overlaid on the temple building?
4. What celestial figure was made inside the temple?
5. What colors were the veil in the temple?
6. How high were the columns at the front of the temple?
7. What were the names Solomon gave to the pillars?
8. What material was used to make the altar?

Answers: (From 2 Chronicles) 1. Moriah (3:1), 2. 60 cubits long, 20 cubits wide (3:3), 3. 600 talents (3:8), 4. Two cherubim (3:10), 5. Blue, purple, and crimson (3:14), 6. 35 cubits (3:15), 7. Right pillar: Jachin, left pillar: Boaz (3:17), 8. Brass (4:1)

772. Who was enlisted to carry the cross for Jesus?
773. These two women stood at the cross as Jesus was crucified.
774. What was Pilate's verdict regarding Jesus?
775. Why was Herod glad to see Jesus brought before him?

Bible Family Trees

776. Who was Jesus' royal relative?
777. Who was the younger brother, Moses or Aaron?
778. This fisherman's two sons became disciples of Jesus.
779. Which of Noah's sons was the father of Canaan?
780. She was "the mother of all living."
781. This cousin of Jesus was the son of the priest Zacharias and Elizabeth.
782. Who was the father of Saul?
783. Who was the grandfather of King David?
784. Which of Isaac's sons was his favorite?
785. How many children did Job have in his later years?

The Early Church

786. Who founded the church at Colosse?
787. What church began at the Pentecost?
788. A helper of Paul, his mother was a Jewish believer and his father was Greek.
789. Who helped Paul establish the church in Corinth?
790. To whom did it fall to take Judas's place among the apostles?

791. This persecutor of Christians was blinded by a heavenly light while on the road to Damascus.
792. Where did Paul preach his first sermon?
793. Who oversaw the church at Jerusalem?
794. God sent this man to restore Saul's sight.
795. A woman named Tabitha, who made clothes for the needy, was also known by this name.

Religious Journeys and Retreats

796. Moses was alone, tending his father-in-law's flock, when the Lord called to him there.
797. Who traveled alone throughout the Judæan wilderness preaching repentance?

BIBLE BRAIN BUSTER

Who had these visions?
1. Ram with two horns
2. Edom's destruction
3. Wheels within wheels
4. The Lord on a throne
5. Jesus' transfiguration
6. A seven-headed beast rising from the sea

Answers: 1. Daniel (Daniel 8:1–3), 2. Obadiah (Obadiah 1), 3. Ezekiel (Ezekiel 1:16), 4. Isaiah (Isaiah 6:1), 5. Peter, James, and John (Matthew 17:9), 6. John (Revelation 13:1)

798. What happened that allowed Joseph to take his family out of Egypt and settle in Nazareth?

799. Jesus went there to fast for forty days and nights, and was tempted by the devil.

800. He saw a vision while beside the river Hiddekel, after fasting for three weeks.

801. The Lord called Elijah to this place, and Elisha insisted on going with him.

802. According to Psalm 9, what will be a refuge for the oppressed?

803. In the book of Amos, what would the people be looking for as they wandered throughout the land?

804. How long did Moses stay on the mountain fasting and talking with God?

805. This man had an amazing vision of the future while in religious exile on the island of Patmos.

Biblical Proportions

806. What were the dimensions of Noah's ark?

807. In John's vision, what was the height, breadth, and length of the holy city?

808. How high was the gallows that Haman had built to hang Mordecai?

809. What were the dimensions of the ark of the covenant?

810. What was the measurement of the wall around the new Jerusalem?

Dreams and Visions

811. This prophet saw a vision of four great beasts that came up from the sea.

812. Who dreamed that the sun, moon, and eleven stars bowed down before him?

813. Who saw a vision of Jesus in heaven while he was being stoned to death?

814. What prophet saw a vision of a field of dry bones?

815. Who dreamed that angels were going up and down a ladder?

816. This man was much troubled by dreams and nightmares.

817. While drinking wine, this king had a vision of a hand writing on a wall.

818. What king had a vision of a tree that grew up to heaven?

819. Who dreamed that he saw seven fat cows and seven thin cows come up out of a river as he stood on the bank?

820. Who saw a vision of God sitting on a throne and holding a book with seven seals in his right hand?

BIBLE BRAIN BUSTER

Fill in the missing letters to find the names of historic Bible locations.

1. S_m_ri_
2. _or_n_h
3. J_ri_ _o
4. P_il_pp_
5. Ga_i_e_

6. Na_a_ _th
7. _gy_t
8. S_n_i
9. _olg_t_a
10. Ar_r_k

Answers: 1. Samaria, 2. Corinth, 3. Jericho, 4. Philippi, 5. Galilee, 6. Nazareth, 7. Egypt, 8. Sinai, 9. Golgotha, 10. Ararak

Prophecies About the Messiah Fulfilled

What New Testament passage fulfills each of these Old Testament prophecies about the Messiah?

821. "So they weighed for my price thirty pieces of silver." *(Zechariah 11:12)*

822. "They part my garments among them, and cast lots upon my vesture." *(Psalm 22:18)*

823. "Behold, a virgin shall conceive, and bear a son, and shall call his name Immanuel." *(Isaiah 7:14)*

824. "He keepeth all his bones: not one of them is broken." *(Psalm 34:20)*

825. "I will open my mouth in a parable." *Psalm 78:2)*

826. "Rejoice greatly, O daughter of Zion: shout, O daughter of Jerusalem: behold, thy King cometh unto thee: he is just, and having salvation: lowly, and riding upon an ass." *(Zechariah 9:9)*

827. "And they shall look upon me whom they have pierced, and they shall mourn . . ." *(Zechariah 12:10)*

828. ". . . And in my thirst they gave me vinegar to drink."

829. "When Israel was a child, then I loved him, and called my son out of Egypt." *(Hosea 11:1)*

830. ". . . He was numbered with the transgressors. . . ." *(Isaiah 53:12)*

Favorite Bible Stories

831. Before the nations began building the tower of Babel, how many languages were there in the world?

832. Why did Moses' mother hide him when he was born?

833. What command did Joshua give to bring the walls of Jericho tumbling down?

834. Ruth married this kinsman-by-marriage after working in his fields.

835. Why was Samson's hair so long?

836. Who watched over Moses, while hidden in the bulrushes?

837. What did Joseph's brothers do with the coat of many colors after selling him to merchants?

838. Who stopped Abraham just as he was about to sacrifice his son Isaac?

839. On what occasion did a multitude of angels sing, "Glory to God in the highest and on earth peace, good will toward men"?

840. David did not set out to kill Goliath. What task had his father given him that fateful day?

841. What did Noah do when he left the ark?

842. What king bowed to political pressure to throw Daniel into the lions' den?

843. In a boat on what lake did Jesus perform the miracle of the fishes?

844. In the parable of the prodigal son, what did the returning youth ask of his father?

845. Who wrestled all night, and was then given a new name?

CHAPTER 7

Bible Inspiration

The world over, people open their Bibles to find hope, comfort, and inspiration. And the Bible is full of so many places to look!

Jesus' Teachings

846. What did Jesus tell the disciples to do if they were not made welcome in a city?
847. How did Jesus say a man can be "born again"?
848. Who did Jesus say would come "in sheep's clothing," but were really "ravening wolves"?
849. Jesus said, "The things which are impossible with men are possible _____."
850. What did Jesus answer when asked if it was lawful to pay taxes to Cæsar?
851. Jesus gave this new commandment to his disciples.
852. In the Sermon on the Mount, what will the merciful receive?

853. Why did Jesus say he had come to the world?

854. What did Jesus tell the disciples to preach to "the lost sheep of the house of Israel"?

855. Who did Jesus say needed his message the most?

856. What will happen to believers "at the last day"?

857. Jesus said, "[A] house divided against itself _____."

858. According to Jesus, what is easier than a rich man entering heaven?

859. Complete this passage: "For what shall it profit a man, if he shall gain the whole world, _____?"

860. Jesus said, "I send you forth as sheep in the midst of wolves: be ye therefore wise as _____ and harmless as _____."

The Book of Psalms

861. Where in the New Testament does this Old Testament verse appear: "Thou art my son, this day I have begotten thee" *(Psalm 2:7)?*

862. In what psalm does David ask forgiveness, saying, "Have mercy upon me, O God, according to thy lovingkindness: according unto the multitude of thy tender mercies blot out my transgressions."

863. What psalm uses the expression, "out of the mouths of babes"?

864. In Psalm 29, God's power is compared to what weather phenomenon?

865. When Jesus spoke the words, "My God, my God, why hast thou forsaken me?" on the cross, what psalm was he quoting?

866. Who wrote Psalm 90?

BIBLE BRAIN BUSTER

Which of these statements about the Book of Psalms are true, and which are false?

1. There are a dozen prophetic psalms that speak of the Messiah.
2. The Book of Psalms is used today by both Jews and Christians.
3. No one knows who wrote the psalms.
4. All of the psalms are songs.
5. "Psalm" is a Greek word meaning "to play a harp."
6. Many of the psalms have directions for musical instruments to accompany them.
7. There are two hundred psalms.
8. The Book of Psalms was a hymnal and prayer book for the Israelite people.

Answers: 1. True: Psalm 2, 8, 16, 22, 40, 45, 68, 69, 72, 97, 110, 118); 2. True; 3. False: David wrote most of them; 4. False: Many are poems; 5. True; 6. True; 7. False (150); 8. True

BIBLE BRAIN BUSTER

Love of the Lord has inspired music and song since ancient times. Try your hand at these musical matchups.

1. They sang the first song mentioned in the Bible.
2. He was the "father of all such as handle the harp and organ."
3. In Psalm 33 it was used to make music.
4. He wrote one thousand and five songs.
5. Prophetess Miriam celebrated a victory by dancing and playing this instrument.
6. In Psalm 137, several of these instruments were hung on poplar trees.
7. This Israelite king had four thousand musicians to praise the Lord.
8. This book of the Bible offers musical direction along with prophecy.

a. Timbrel
b. Ten-stringed lyre
c. Jubal
d. Solomon
e. Harps
f. Moses and children of Israel
g. David
h. Habakkuk

Answers: 1. f (Exodus 15:1), 2. c (Genesis 4:21), 3. b (Psalm 33:2), 4. d (1 Kings 4:30-32), 5. a (Exodus 15:20), 6. e (Psalm 137:2), 7. g (1 Chronicles 23:5), 8. h (Habakkuk 3:1, 3, 9, 13, 19)

867. Which psalm says, "The Lord is my rock, and my fortress, and my deliverer; my God, my strength, in whom I will trust"?

868. In which psalm does David express such happiness that the hills rejoice and the valleys shout with joy?

869. Which musical instruments does Psalm 150 say to use in praise of the Lord?

870. Which psalm of celebration begins, "Make a joyful noise unto the Lord, all ye lands"?

871. The verse, "The mountains skipped like rams, and the little hills like lambs" is from what psalm?

872. According to Psalm 15, who shall abide in God's tabernacle?

873. In what psalm does Asaph admit that he was jealous because the wicked seemed to have a happy and prosperous life?

874. The words "They that sow in tears shall reap in joy" appear in what psalm?

875. Which psalm of David begins, "The Lord is my light and my salvation; whom shall I fear? the Lord is the strength of my life; of whom shall I be afraid?"

BIBLE BRAIN BUSTER

Who made each of these biblical promises?
1. That no one would die if they ate a piece of fruit
2. To hide spies if her life was spared
3. That the Israelites wouldn't leave Egypt empty-handed
4. His daughter's hand in marriage to the man who could capture Kirjath-sepher
5. His birthright for a bowl of soup
6. Money and a wife to the man who killed the giant from Gath
7. Power and glory in return for worship
8. One-tenth of all God would give him, in return for God's protection

Answers: 1. Serpent (Genesis 3:4), 2. Rahab (Joshua 2:3, 14), 3. God (Exodus 3:15–21), 4. Caleb (Joshua 15:16–17), 5. Esau (Genesis 25:33–34), 6. Saul (1 Samuel 17:25), 7. The Devil (Luke 4:6–7), 8. Jacob (Genesis 28:20–22)

Wise Proverbs

Fill in the blanks to complete these wise proverbs:

876. "A soft answer turneth away_____."
877. "_____doeth good like a medicine."
878. "He that spareth his _____ hateth his son: but he that loveth him chasteneth him betimes."

879. "The way of the wicked is an abomination unto the Lord: but he loveth him that followeth after _____."

880. "Go to the _____, thou sluggard; consider her ways, and be wise."

881. "Let another man _____ thee, and not thine own mouth."

882. "A word fitly spoken is like _____ of gold in pictures of silver."

883. "Wealth gotten by vanity shall be diminished: but he that gathereth by _____ shall increase."

884. "Heaviness in the heart of man maketh it stoop: but a good word _____."

885. "_____ in the Lord with all thine heart."

BIBLE BRAIN BUSTER

Who prayed in each of these places?

1. In an upstairs room
2. In a tower
3. On a sick bed
4. On street corners
5. In a garden
6. Inside a big fish
7. In a prison
8. At a window

Answers: 1. Jesus (Luke 22:16–22), 2. Habakkuk (Habakkuk 2:1), 3. Hezekiah (2 Kings 20:1–7), 4. Hypocrites (Matthew 6:5), 5. Jesus (Mark 14:32–36, 6. Jonah (Jonah 2:1), 7. Paul and Silas (Acts 16:23–25), 8. Daniel (Daniel 6:10–11)

The Parables of Jesus

886. Before the good Samaritan finally stopped to help him, who passed by a robbed and injured man?

887. What did the man do, who lost only one of his one hundred sheep?

888. What idea was Jesus illustrating with the parable of the householder and his laborers?

889. Who said that it was right to have a party because "this thy brother was dead, and is alive again; and was lost, and is found"?

890. Which ten women appeared in a parable about being prepared for the arrival of the Son of man?

891. In the parable of the sower and the seeds, what did the seeds that fell on fertile ground and produced fruit symbolize?

892. In a parable that teaches the wisdom of humility, what two men went to the temple to pray?

893. In another parable, to whom does Jesus say, "Ask, and it shall be given you; seek, and ye shall find; knock, and it shall be opened unto you."

894. Which parable ends with the lesson, "Many are called, but few are chosen"?

895. Which supposedly barren fruit tree does Jesus use in a parable to show that people should be given a chance to repent?

Ecclesiastes and the Song of Solomon

896. What does the author call the Song of Solomon?

897. "To every thing there is a season, and _____."

898. What sweet foods of the wedding feast are mentioned in chapter five of the Song of Solomon?

899. "A good name is better than _____."

900. Who is the author of Ecclesiastes?

901. In what season is the Song of Solomon set?

902. Although generations of humankind come and go, what does the author of Ecclesiastes say "abideth forever"?

903. Whose courtship and marriage does the Song of Solomon celebrate?

904. In the Song of Solomon, "My love among the daughters" is compared to this.

905. "A time to weep, and a time to _____; a time to mourn, and a time to _____."

Faith, Hope, and Charity

906. "And now abideth faith, hope, charity, these three; but the greatest of these is _____."

907. What did Jesus say could move mountains?

908. Name the book of the Bible where you can find

these words: "Happy is he that hath the God of Jacob for his help, whose hope is in the Lord his God."

909. Who wrote in a letter, "The prayer of faith shall save the sick, and the Lord shall raise him up"?

910. Who said, "I know thy works, and charity, and service, and faith, and thy patience, and thy works; and the last to be more than the first"?

911. Which epistle tells believers to put on "the breastplate of faith and love," and the "helmet [of] the hope of salvation"?

912. In the face of suffering, what continues to give hope?

913. What makes faith perfect?

914. Who wrote, "Charity suffereth long, and is kind; charity envieth not; charity vaunteth not itself, is not puffed up"?

915. Which prophet wrote, "Behold, his soul which is lifted up is not upright in him: but the just shall live by his faith"?

It's a Miracle

The Bible is filled with miraculous happenings from beginning to end, but if you know your Bible well, it won't take a miracle to answer all of these questions correctly!

916. What happened to Aaron's staff in the tabernacle?
917. During a battle, the Lord answered Joshua's prayer with this miracle over Gibeon.
918. After healing two blind men, what did Jesus tell them not to do?
919. Which apostle got to walk on water for a short time?
920. Which bird did God send to feed the Israelites in the wilderness?
921. Who did Elisha raise from the dead by stretching out on his body?
922. How did the woman who suffered from an "issue of blood" get cured?
923. What did Elisha's messenger tell Naaman he must do to be cured of leprosy?
924. Whose hand suddenly became leprous, and then was healed again?
925. Who did Peter heal of palsy?
926. After the Resurrection, what was Jesus able to walk through?
927. What was the first miracle Jesus performed?
928. Who healed Eutychus after he fell from a window and died?
929. How were the Israelites healed of snakebite?
930. Who appeared and talked with Jesus at the Transfiguration?
931. Whose rod turned into a serpent, and swal-

lowed the sorcerer's serpents?

932. In Ephesus, what happened when Paul placed his hands on believers?

933. What was Jesus doing just before he calmed the stormy sea?

934. Why did people say Jesus shouldn't have healed the woman who was stooped over?

935. How did God stop the Egyptians' chariots from advancing?

936. How did Jesus heal Peter's mother-in-law of a fever?

937. Peter raised this woman from the dead.

938. In what city did Jesus heal a demon-possessed man in the synagogue?

939. Where did Jesus raise Lazarus from the dead?

940. What miracle occurred when a dead man's body touched Elisha's bones?

Heavenly Messengers

941. Which angel appeared to Joshua near Jericho?

942. Who was sent by an angel on a missionary journey to the south?

943. An angel visited this man's mother and told her that her son would be a Nazarite.

944. What kind of angels did God send to guard the entrance to the Garden of Eden?

BIBLE BRAIN BUSTER

Special observances remind us to keep God alive in our hearts. Name the ritual, symbol, or religious observance that commemorates each of the following.

1. The Jew's salvation from Haman
2. The completion of God's creation
3. The body and blood of Christ
4. The Israelites' simple homes in Egypt
5. The angel of death taking the firstborn of Egypt
6. The passing of the Israelites over the Jordan

Answers: 1. Purim (Esther 9:28), 2. Sabbath (Genesis 2:3), 3. The Lord's Supper (Luke 22:19), 4. Feast of Tabernacles (Succoth) (Leviticus 23:39–43), 5. Passover (Exodus 12:11–14), 6. The twelve stones (Joshua 4:1–6)

945. This cousin of Jesus was named by an angel.

946. What was the name of the angel who appeared to Zacharias and Mary?

947. Who had an angel prepare meals for him?

948. This man was stopped by an angel from sacrificing his child.

949. What kind of angel did Isaiah see praising God in the temple?

950. How many angels were sent to save Lot and his family during the destruction of Sodom?

951. Where was Jesus praying when an angel came

and gave him strength?

952. Which angel helped Daniel understand his vision of the future?

953. An angel will bind Satan with this at the end of time.

954. Which prophet saw the Lord's angel riding upon a red horse?

955. How many angels will be at the gates of the New Jerusalem?

Letters and Epistles

Even in ancient times, written correspondence played an important part in people's lives. Answer these questions about famous letters and their authors.

956. After receiving a letter from this warring king, Hezekiah turned to God for help and guidance.

957. This letter-writer called himself "the apostle of the Gentiles."

958. For whom did John "take a letter" to seven churches?

959. Who wrote a letter of recommendation for Paul and sent it to Felix the governor?

960. Who wrote a letter to King Jehoram warning him of punishment from God for leading his people in the ways of evil?

BIBLE BRAIN BUSTER

People look to God for answers—and sometimes God asks things of us. Match each of these questions to the questioner.

1. "O Lord my God, hast thou also brought evil upon the widow with whom I sojourn, by slaying her son?"

2. "Alas, O Lord God, wherefore hast thou at all brought this people over Jordan, to deliver us into the hand of the Amorites, to destroy us?"

3. "What is this that thou hast done?"

4. "For who is able to judge this thy so great a people?"

5. "Who am I, that I should go unto Pharaoh, and that I should bring forth the children of Israel out of Egypt?"

6. "Shall I go and smite these Philistines?"

a. Solomon
b. God
c. Elijah
d. David
e. Moses
f. Joshua

Answers: 1. c (1 Kings 17:20), 2. f (Joshua 7:7), 3. b (Genesis 3:13), 4. a (1 Kings 3:9), 5. e (Exodus 3:11), 6. d (1 Samuel 23:1–2)

961. Who wrote the first letter to the church at Corinth?

962. This man, a leper, delivered a letter to the king of Israel from the king of Syria.

963. Paul told this church to share his letter with the church of Laodicea.

964. Who wrote a letter to Philemon on behalf of a runaway slave named Onesimus?

965. What message did David send to Joab in a letter?

966. This woman wrote letters about Naboth in her husband's name and sent them to the leaders of Jezreel.

967. Who wrote a letter of recommendation for Apollos when he went to Corinth?

968. Who wrote to "the strangers scattered throughout Pontus, Galatia, Cappadocia, Asia, and Bithynia"?

969. Which persecutor of Christians went to the high priest to ask for letters of introduction to the synagogues in Damascus?

970. Who wrote letters that resulted in the beheading of Ahab's seventy sons?

Praise and Prayer

Prayer is characterized by one or more of the

following elements: petition, confession, praise, and thanksgiving. Who is praying in each of these verses?

971. "Evening and morning, and at noon, will I pray, and cry aloud: and he shall hear my voice."

972. "And he kneeled down, and cried with a loud voice, Lord, lay not this sin to their charge. And when he had said this, he fell asleep."

973. "Lord God, what wilt thou give me, seeing I go childless . . . Behold, to me thou hast given no seed: and, lo, one born in my house is mine heir."

974. "My soul doth magnify the Lord, And my spirit hath rejoiced in God my Savior. For he hath regarded the low estate of his handmaiden: for, behold, from henceforth all generations shall call me blessed."

975. "Father, the hour is come: glorify thy Son, that thy Son also may glorify thee."

976. "I beseech thee, shew me thy glory."

977. "Lord, remember me when thou comest into thy kingdom."

978. "And at midnight . . . prayed, and sang praises unto God: and the prisoners heard them. And suddenly there was a great earthquake, so that the foundations of the prison were shaken."

979. "O Lord God of Israel . . . bow down thine ear,

and hear: open, Lord, thine eyes, and see: and hear the words of Sennacherib, which hath sent him to reproach the living God."

980. "I am cast out of thy sight; yet I will look again toward thy holy temple."

981. "Give us this day our daily bread. And forgive us our debts, as we forgive our debtors."

982. "For thou art my rock and my fortress; therefore for thy name's sake lead me, and guide me. Pull me out of the net that they have laid privily for me: for thou art my strength."

983. "For this child I prayed; and the Lord hath given me my petition which I asked of him: Therefore also I have lent him to the Lord; as long as he liveth he shall be lent to the Lord."

984. "O my Father, if this cup may not pass away from me, except I drink it, thy will be done."

985. "There was given to me a thorn in the flesh, the messenger of Satan to buffet me, lest I should be exalted above measure. For this thing I besought the Lord thrice, that it might depart from me."

986. "Hear me, O Lord, hear me, that this people may know that thou art the Lord God. . . . Then the fire of the Lord fell, and consumed the burnt sacrifice, and the wood, and the

stones, and the dust, and licked up the water that was in the trench."

987. ". . . And kneeled down, and prayed; and turning him to the body said, Tabitha arise. And she opened her eyes. . . . "

988. "I have sinned greatly in that I have done: and now, I beseech thee, O Lord, take away the iniquity of thy servant; for I have done very foolishly."

989. "Wherefore I abhor myself, and repent in dust and ashes."

990. "Who is like unto thee, O Lord, among the gods? who is like thee, glorious in holiness, fearful in praises, doing wonders?"

Bible Promises and Covenants

Complete each of these biblical covenants or promises.

991. "If ye abide in me, and my words abide in you, ye shall ask what ye will, and _____."

992. "I do set my _____ in the cloud, and it shall be for a token of a covenant between me and the earth."

993. "And I will bring you in unto the _____, concerning the which I did swear to give it to

Abraham, to Isaac, and to Jacob; and I will give it you for an heritage: I am the Lord."

994. "The daughter of Herodias danced before them, and pleased Herod. Whereupon he promised with an oath to give her _____."

995. "Behold, my covenant is with thee, and thou shalt be a father of _____."

996. "Verily I say unto thee, To-day shalt thou be with me in _____."

997. "And he declared unto you his covenant, which he commanded you to perform, even _____; and he wrote them upon two tables of stone."

998. "Blessed are the peacemakers: for they shall be called the _____."

999. "Thy wife Elizabeth shall bear thee a son, and thou shalt call his name _____."

1000. He that believeth and is baptized shall be _____."

CHAPTER 8

Just for Kids

Okay, kids, it's your turn! Let's see how much you know about the Bible, from the story of creation to the Resurrection of Christ.

1. How many days did it take for God to create the whole world?
2. Why did Adam and Eve hide from God in the garden?
3. What were the names of Adam and Eve's sons?
4. Why did God choose Noah to build the ark?
5. How long did the rain last?
6. What was God's sign to Noah that the earth would never again be destroyed by a flood?
7. During the building of what tower did the Lord make all the nations speak different languages?
8. What did God promise Abraham and Sarah?
9. What did the angels tell Lot and his family *not* to do?

10. Who was Isaac's wife?
11. Who had a dream about angels walking up and down a ladder?
12. What gift did Jacob give to his son Joseph?
13. Joseph explained the dreams of what ruler?

BIBLE BRAIN BUSTER

Unscramble these Bible names.

1. HAON
2. MADA
3. THRU
4. RAMY
5. TREEP
6. NOJHA
7. BOJ
8. LEANID
9. SOPHEJ
10. DREOH

Answers: 1. Noah, 2. Adam, 3. Ruth, 4. Mary, 5. Peter, 6. Jonah, 7. Job, 8. Daniel, 9. Joseph, 10. Herod

14. How did Moses' mother save his life?
15. How did God call to Moses?
16. At the Red Sea, what miracle saved the Israelite people from the Egyptian soldiers?
17. What is the first of the Ten Commandments?
18. What did the Israelites call the special tent where they worshiped God?
19. What leader won the battle of Jericho?
20. God helped this man and a small army of soldiers defeat the Midianites.

21. What did Delilah do that made Samson lose his strength?
22. This woman loved her mother-in-law so much, she wouldn't leave her.
23. Who was the first king of Israel?
24. What did David do to make King Saul feel better when he was troubled?
25. What did young David use to kill the giant Goliath?
26. This wise king settled a fight over a baby.
27. What special place did King Solomon have built?
28. What prophet of God stayed beside a brook and had his food brought to him by ravens?
29. Who was Elijah's helper?
30. Where did the whirlwind take Elijah?
31. This Jewish woman saved her people from the plot of an evil man named Haman.

BIBLE BRAIN BUSTER

Name the missing letter in each of these Bible places.

1. Eg_pt
2. B_thl_h_m
3. Jer_cho

4. E_en
5. Jo_dan
6. Jer_salem

Answers: 1. y, 2. e, 3. i, 4. d, 5. r, 6. u

BIBLE BRAIN BUSTER

Name the number that goes with each of these biblical events.

1. The animals went onto the ark ___ by___.
2. Jonah was in the belly of the big fish for ___ days and___ nights.
3. God rested on day number ___.
4. Peter denied Jesus ___ times.
5. Jesus had ___ disciples.

Answers: 1. two, 2. three, 3. seven, 4. three, 5. twelve

32. This man suffered greatly, but never lost his faith in God.

33. Which psalm begins, "The Lord is my shepherd; I shall not want"?

34. When this man was thrown into the lions' den, an angel came and saved him.

35. Which prophet was thrown overboard into the sea during a terrible storm, and then swallowed by a big fish?

36. What did the angel Gabriel tell Mary?

37. In what city was Jesus born?

38. Where did Jesus sleep his first night on earth?

39. Who came to visit the baby Jesus, bringing gold, frankincense, and myrrh?

40. Where did Jesus' family live?

41. Where was young Jesus when his parents could not find him?
42. Where did Jesus go to be baptized by John the Baptist?
43. Who tempted Jesus when he was in the wilderness?
44. How many apostles did Jesus have?
45. Which king had John the Baptist beheaded?
46. Which apostle's name means "rock"?
47. With what miracle did Jesus feed five thousand-people?
48. In one parable, who stopped to help a man when everyone else just walked on by?
49. Which miracle did Jesus perform for Lazarus?
50. Who did Jesus throw out of the temple?

BIBLE BRAIN BUSTER

Match the children on the left with their Bible parents on the right.

1. John the Baptist
2. Cain and Abel
3. Isaac
4. Jesus

a. Sarah and Abraham
b. Mary and Joseph
c. Adam and Eve
d. Elizabeth and Zacharias

Answers: 1. d, 2. c, 3. a, 4. b

51. At the Last Supper, what did Jesus tell the disciples to eat and drink in remembrance of him?
52. What special thing did Jesus do for the disciples after supper?
53. Which disciple betrayed Jesus?
54. Jesus was brought to trial in front of what Roman governor?
55. Before they crucified him, what did the soldiers put on Jesus' head?
56. What was the name of the place where Jesus was crucified?
57. How did the soldiers seal Jesus' tomb?
58. Who was the first person to see Jesus after the Resurrection?
59. Who doubted that Jesus had risen, at first?
60. Who watched as Jesus rose up into heaven?

Answers to Chapter 8:
Just for Kids

1. Six—he rested on the seventh. *(Genesis 1:21)*
2. They had disobeyed God *(Genesis 3:8–12)*
3. Cain and Abel *(Genesis 4:1–2)*
4. Because Noah was a good man *(Genesis 6:8)*
5. Forty days and forty nights *(Genesis 7:4)*
6. A rainbow *(Genesis 9:11–13)*
7. Babel *(Genesis 11:1–9)*
8. That they would have a son *(Genesis 15:5)*
9. Look back *(Genesis 19:17)*
10. Rebekah *(Genesis 24:15–51)*
11. Jacob *(Genesis 28:10–12)*
12. A coat of many colors *(Genesis 37:3)*
13. Pharaoh *(Genesis 41:15)*
14. She hid him in the bulrushes *(Exodus 2:3)*
15. From a burning bush *(Exodus 3:2)*
16. The parting of the waters *(Exodus 14:21)*
17. "Thou shalt have no other gods before me." *(Exodus 20:3)*
18. The Tabernacle *(Exodus 26:1)*

19. Joshua *(Joshua 6)*
20. Gideon *(Judges 7:19–25)*
21. Cut his hair *(Judges 16:19)*
22. Ruth *(Ruth 2:16)*
23. Saul *(1 Samuel 15–17)*
24. He played the harp *(1 Samuel 16:23)*
25. A sling and a stone *(1 Samuel 17:50)*
26. Solomon *(1 Kings 3:16–28)*
27. The temple *(1 Kings 5-7)*
28. Elijah *(1 Kings 17:4)*
29. Elisha *(1 Kings 19:16)*
30. To heaven *(2 Kings 2:11)*
31. Esther *(The Book of Esther)*
32. Job *(The Book of Job)*
33. Psalm 23
34. Daniel *(Daniel 6:16–22)*
35. Jonah *(Jonah 1:15–17)*
36. That she would have a son named Jesus *(Luke 1:26–31)*
37. Bethlehem *(Luke 2:3–6)*
38. In a manger *(Luke 2:7)*
39. Three wise men *(Matthew 2:1)*
40. Nazareth *(Matthew 2:23)*
41. In the temple *(Luke 2:46)*
42. The river Jordan *(Matthew 4:13)*
43. The devil *(Matthew 4:1)*
44. Twelve *(Luke 9:1)*

45. Herod *(Mark 6:22–27)*
46. Peter *(Matthew 16:18)*
47. "Loaves and fishes" *(Mark 6:38–42)*
48. The good Samaritan *(Luke 10:33)*
49. He raised him from the dead *(John 11:43–44)*
50. The moneychangers *(Matthew 21:12–13)*
51. Bread and wine *(Matthew 26:26–28)*
52. Washed their feet *(John 13:4–5)*
53. Judas *(Mark 14:43–46)*
54. Pontius Pilate *(Mark 15:1)*
55. A crown of thorns *(Mark 15:17)*
56. Golgotha *(Matthew 27:33)*
57. With a stone *(Matthew 28:66)*
58. Mary Magdalene *(Mark 16:9)*
59. Thomas *(John 21:26–29)*
60. The apostles *(Acts 1:9)*

THE ANSWERS

The Answers

Chapter 1—Flexing Your Bible Trivia Muscles

1. The dust of the ground *(Genesis 2:7)*
2. Brimstone and fire *(Genesis 19:24)*
3. John the Baptist *(Matthew 3:2)*
4. A mustard seed *(Mark 4:30–32)*
5. An angel of God closed their mouths. *(Daniel 6:22)*
6. Aaron and his sons *(Leviticus 8:23)*
7. Peter *(Matthew 17:24–27)*
8. Job *(Job 1:21)*
9. Peter *(Matthew 16:18)*
10. Joppa *(Jonah 1:3)*
11. One *(Luke 17:11–19)*
12. Destruction *and* a haughty spirit *(Proverbs 16:18)*
13. Zipporah *(Exodus 2:21)*
14. Ruth *(Ruth 1:16)*
15. He was too short to see above the crowd. *(Luke 19:2–5)*
16. David *(1 Samuel 17:39–40)*
17. For they shall see God *(Matthew 5:8)*

18. Solomon *(1 Kings 3:16–28)*
19. The pale horse *(Revelation 6:8)*
20. Murder *(Exodus 20:13)*
21. Ten *(Exodus 7:17, 11:5)*
22. The ant *(Proverbs 6:6)*
23. An angel touched his lips with a live coal from the altar *(Isaiah 6:4–7)*
24. A rainbow *(Genesis 9:13–15)*
25. Psalm 23
26. Simon *(Matthew 10:2)*
27. Daniel *(Daniel 2:16–48)*
28. Gideon *(Judges 8:30)*
29. Lot *(Genesis 19:26)*
30. Onesimus *(Philemon)*
31. The prodigal son *(Luke 15:28)*
32. The devil *(Luke 4:3)*
33. Egypt *(Matthew 2:13)*
34. Pilate *(Luke 23:4)*
35. Esau *(Genesis 25:33)*
36. Peter *(Acts 9:33)*
37. Two angels *(Genesis 19:1–22)*
38. Zechariah *(Zechariah 9:9)*
39. By playing the harp *(1 Samuel 16:23)*
40. Fish *(Luke 24:38–43)*
41. Job *(Job 1:20)*
42. Saul *(1 Samuel 31:5)*
43. An angel told him *(Matthew 1:20–21)*

44. The lion of the tribe of Judah *(Revelation 5:5)*
45. Noah *(Genesis 8:6–12)*
46. Bathsheba *(2 Samuel 11:2–3)*
47. Micaiah *(2 Chronicles 18:18)*
48. Orpah *(Ruth 1:4)*
49. Beside Jacob's well, in Samaria *(John 4:5–15)*
50. As a reminder of how God fed the people in the wilderness *(Exodus 16:32)*

Chapter 2—People in the Bible

Who Was It?

51. Joseph *(Genesis 37:28)*
52. Stephen *(Acts 7:59)*
53. Elijah *(2 Kings 2:11)*
54. God *(Genesis 2:8)*
55. Nadab and Abihu *(Leviticus 10:1–2)*
56. Jotham *(2 Kings 15:32–38)*
57. Rahab *(Joshua 2:15–21)*
58. Abraham *(Genesis 12:1–9)*
59. Adam and Eve *(Genesis 3:23)*
60. Bartimaeus *(Luke 18:35–42)*
61. Stephen *(Acts 7:60)*
62. Paul *(Acts 19)*
63. Andrew *(Matthew 10:2)*
64. Zerubbabel *(Ezra 4)*

65. Nehemiah *(Nehemiah 1:1)*
66. Jairus *(Luke 8:40–56)*
67. Jonah *(Jonah 2:1)*
68. Hosea *(Hosea 1:2–3)*
69. Esther *(Esther 5:4)*
70. Malachi *(Malachi 2:16)*
71. Simon of Cyrene *(Mark 15:21)*
72. Thomas *(John 20:24–29)*
73. Aaron *(Exodus 7:1)*
74. Martha *(Luke 10:38–39)*
75. Mordecai *(Esther 2:5)*
76. Hur *(Exodus 17:12)*
77. Delilah *(Judges 16:4–5)*
78. Balaam *(Numbers 23:5)*
79. Solomon *(1 Kings 5:1–6)*
80. Joseph of Arimathea *(Luke 23:50–53)*
81. Josiah *(2 Chronicles 34:1)*
82. Silas *(Acts 15:22)*
83. Haman *(Esther 3:1)*
84. Abel *(Genesis 4:2)*
85. Elizabeth *(Luke 1:13)*
86. Cæsar Augustus *(Luke 2:1)*
87. Tabitha *(Acts 9:36)*
88. Potiphar *(Genesis 37:36)*
89. Habakkuk *(Habakkuk 3:19)*
90. James *(Matthew 13:55)*
91. Isaac *(Genesis 17:19)*

92. Ezekiel *(Ezekiel 1:3)*
93. Samuel *(1 Samuel 3:19–20)*
94. Miriam *(Exodus 15:20)*
95. Ruth *(Ruth 4:10)*
96. Zedekiah *(2 Chronicles 36:10)*
97. A wise woman of Tekoa *(2 Samuel 14:1–23)*
98. Dinah *(Genesis 30:21)*
99. Barabbas *(Matthew 27:16)*
100. Cain *(Genesis 4:1)*
101. Jacob *(Genesis 25:26)*
102. Simon *(Matthew 10:4)*
103. Phoebe *(Romans 16:1–2)*
104. Herodias *(Mark 6:18-19)*
105. Ahab *(1 Kings 16:31)*

Who Said That?

106. Nahum *(Nahum 1:3)*
107. God *(Numbers 6:24)*
108. Solomon *(Proverbs 8:11)*
109. Paul *(2 Corinthians 9:7)*
110. Paul *(Galatians 6:7)*
111. Job *(Job 17:1)*
112. God *(Zephaniah 1:13)*
113. Jesus *(John 19:11)*
114. John *(Revelation 21:1)*
115. The serpent *(Genesis 3:4)*
116. Peter *(Mark 14:29)*

117. Jesus *(Luke 9:24)*
118. Solomon *(Song of Solomon 2:2)*
119. Jacob *(Genesis 28:22)*
120. James *(James 2:20)*
121. Moses *(Exodus 32:12)*
122. Moses *(Exodus 16:15)*
123. Daniel *(Daniel 9:3)*
124. God *(Joshua 1:5)*
125. Peter *(Matthew 14.28)*
126. David *(2 Samuel 19:4)*
127. Pharaoh *(Exodus 5:2)*
128. Nebuchadnezzar *(Daniel 4:5)*
129. Nicodemus *(John 3:2)*
130. John the Baptist *(Matthew 3:14)*
131. Isaiah *(Isaiah 7:14)*
132. Eve *(Genesis 3:13)*
133. Cain *(Genesis 4:13)*
134. Elijah *(1 Kings 18:21)*
135. Peter *(Acts 2:38)*
136. Hezekiah *(2 Kings 20:8)*
137. Pharaoh's daughter *(Exodus 2:6)*
138. Mary *(Luke 1:38)*
139. Rehoboam *(1 Kings 12:14)*
140. Goliath *(1 Samuel 17:43)*
141. Naomi *(Ruth 1:11)*
142. Miriam *(Exodus 2:7)*
143. Athaliah *(2 Kings 11:14)*

144. Herod *(Matthew 14:2)*

145. Joseph's brothers *(Genesis 42:11)*

What's in a Name?

146. Simon or Simeon *(John 1:42)*

147. Saul *(Acts 13:9)*

148. Mattaniah *(2 Kings 24:17)*

149. Abram *(Genesis 17:5)*

150. Sarai *(Genesis 17: 15)*

151. Jedidiah *(2 Samuel 12:24–25)*

152. Jacob *(Genesis 32:28)*

153. Oshea *(Numbers 13:16)*

154. Eliakim *(2 Kings 23:34)*

155. Daniel *(Daniel 1:6–7)*

Husbands and Wives, Sons and Daughters

156. Abigail *(1 Samuel 25:18–20)*

157. Rizpah *(2 Samuel 21:1–10)*

158. Aholibamah *(Genesis 36:2, 5)*

159. Adah and Zillah *(Genesis 4:19–24)*

160. Esau *(Genesis 26:24, 28:9)*

161. Hannah *(1 Samuel 2:19)*

162. The woman at the well *(John 4:6–19)*

163. Herod *(Mark 6:17)*

164. The church *(Revelation 19:7–9)*

165. Rehoboam *(2 Chronicles 11:21)*

166. Eli *(1 Samuel 3:13)*

167. Jacob *(Genesis 29:15–25)*
168. Asenath *(Genesis 41:45)*
169. Tamar *(Genesis 38:6–10)*
170. Esther *(Esther 2:7)*
171. Lot *(Genesis 19:30)*
172. Noah *(Genesis 10)*
173. Mary and Joseph *(Luke 2:46–49)*
174. The daughter of Herodias *(Matthew 14:6–8)*
175. Hashubah *(1 Chronicles 3:20)*
176. Meshullemeth *(2 Kings 21:19)*
177. Drusilla *(Acts 24:24)*
178. Hashem *(1 Chronicles 11:34)*
179. Benjamin *(Genesis 42:4)*
180. Jochebed *(Exodus 6:20)*

Bible Rulers

181. Abimelech *(Judges 9:6)*
182. Hezekiah *(2 Kings 20:5–6)*
183. David *(1 Samuel 16:6–13)*
184. Herod *(Luke 13:32)*
185. Eglon *(Judges 3:15–30)*
186. Josiah *(2 Chronicles 34:31–33)*
187. Joseph *(Genesis 41:1–40)*
188. Jehoiakim *(Jeremiah 26:20–23)*
189. Sihon *(Numbers 21:21–26)*
190. Cæsar Augustus *(Luke 2:1)*
191. Ahaziah *(2 Kings 1:2)*

192. Belshazzar *(Daniel 5:1–9)*
193. Abimelech *(Genesis 20:2)*
194. Herod *(Matthew 2:16)*
195. The Queen of Sheba *(1 Kings 10:1–13)*
196. Jabin *(Judges 4:2–3)*
197. Jehoram *(2 Kings 8:16–18)*
198. Artaxerxes *(Nehemiah 2:1–5)*
199. Manasseh *(2 Chronicles 33:10–13)*
200. Ethbaal *(1 Kings 16:31)*
201. Elah *(1 Kings 16:8–10)*
202. David *(2 Samuel 24:25)*
203. Herod *(Matthew 14:3–10)*
204. Cushan-Rishathaim *(Judges 3:8)*
205. Ahab *(1 Kings 16:29–33)*
206. Nebuchadnezzar *(Daniel 4:10–18)*
207. Agrippa *(Acts 26)*
208. Darius *(Ezra 6:1, 8)*
209. Saul *(1 Samuel 18:10–11)*
210. Agag *(1 Samuel 15:8, 32)*
211. Josiah *(2 Kings 22:8–10)*
212. Herod *(Luke 23:8)*
213. Ahasuerus *(Esther 3:1)*
214. Joram, king of Israel; Jehoshaphat of Judah; and the king of Edom *(2 Kings 3:11–19)*
215. Zachariah *(2 Kings 15:8–10)*
216. Darius *(Daniel 6)*
217. Azariah *(2 Kings 15:1–5)*

218. Hoshea *(2 Kings 17:1–4)*
219. Josiah *(2 Chronicles 35: 23-25)*
220. Solomon *(2 Chronicles 2:1)*
221. Solomon *(Song of Songs 1:1)*
222. David *(2 Samuel 12:1-15)*
223. The king of Edom *(Numbers 20:14–20)*
224. Melchizedek *(Genesis 14:18)*
225. Mesha *(2 Kings 3:4)*
226. Herod *(Acts 12:1–3)*
227. Zedekiah *(2 Kings 25:1–7)*
228. Og *(Deuteronomy 3:11)*
229. Ahab *(1 Kings 22:17)*
230. Pilate *(John 19:21)*

Women of the Bible

231. Herodias *(Matthew 14:3–8)*
232. Rachel *(Genesis 35:18)*
233. Anna *(Luke 2:36–38)*
234. Dinah *(Genesis 34:1)*
235. Elizabeth *(Luke 1:5)*
236. The Samaritan woman *(John 4:15)*
237. Rahab *(Joshua 2, 6)*
238. Mary and Martha *(John 11:32–39)*
239. Euodias and Syntyche *(Philippians 4:2)*
240. Aholibamah *(Genesis 36:2)*
241. Abigail *(1 Samuel 25:18)*
242. Leah *(Genesis 29:31)*

243. The wise woman of Tekoah *(2 Samuel 14:2–5)*
244. Tamar *(Genesis 38:13–15)*
245. Tahpenes *(1 Kings 11:19)*
246. Esther *(Esther 8:7)*
247. Potiphar's wife *(Genesis 39:14)*
248. Bathsheba *(2 Samuel 11–12)*
249. Miriam *(Exodus 15, Numbers 12)*
250. Asenath *(Genesis 46:20)*
251. Rizpah *(2 Samuel 3:7)*
252. Martha *(John 11:24–26)*
253. The daughter of Herodias *(Matthew 14:1–11)*
254. Jael *(Judges 4)*
255. Bernice *(Acts 25:13)*
256. Naomi *(Ruth 1:3–5)*
257. Elizabeth *(Luke 1:36)*
258. Sapphira *(Acts 5:5–10)*
259. Orpah *(Ruth 1:4)*
260. Anna *(Luke 2:36)*
261. Deborah *(Judges 4–5)*
262. Salome *(Mark 15:40)*
263. Rebekah *(Genesis 27)*
264. The witch of Endor *(1 Samuel 28)*
265. Jezebel *(2 Kings 9:30–37)*
266. Huldah *(2 Kings 22:14–20)*
267. Adah and Zillah *(Genesis 4:19–24)*
268. Hagar *(Genesis 16:1)*
269. The mother of his disciple Peter *(Mark 1:30–31)*

141

270. Mary *(Luke 10:39–42)*
271. Bathsheba *(2 Samuel 11:1–3)*
272. Vashti *(Esther 1:19)*
273. Candace *(Acts 8:27)*
274. Maachah *(1 Kings 15:13)*
275. Michal *(1 Samuel 18:27)*
276. Tahpenes *(1 Kings 11:19)*
277. Esther, Ruth
278. Rebekah *(Genesis 24:15–51)*
279. Lydia *(Acts 16:11–15)*
280. Mary and Mary Magdalene *(Mark 16:9–13)*

Heroes and Villains

281. Haman *(Esther 3:8–13)*
282. Stephen *(Acts 7:55–59)*
283. Samson *(Judges 16:29–31)*
284. Moses *(Exodus 3:6–10)*
285. Joseph *(Genesis 41:45–49, 54–57)*
286. Esther *(Book of Esther)*
287. Joshua *(Joshua 6:20)*
288. David *(1 Samuel 17:50–52)*
289. Jezebel *(1 Kings 19:1–3)*
290. Judas *(Matthew 26:48, 27:3–10)*

Bible Children

291. Jacob *(Genesis 27:18–37)*
292. Cain *(Genesis 4:8–10)*

293. Ham *(Genesis 9:18–24)*
294. Benjamin *(Genesis 35:16–18)*
295. Ephraim *(Genesis 41:51–52)*
296. Jacob and Esau *(Genesis 25:23–26)*
297. Jair *(Judges 10:3–4)*
298. Younger *(Luke 15:11–32)*
299. Heman *(1 Chronicles 25:5)*
300. David *(1 Chronicles 3:1–9)*
301. Jairus's daughter *(Luke 8:40–56)*
302. Samuel *(1 Samuel 1:26–28)*
303. A young Israelite girl captured in battle *(2 Kings 5:2–3)*
304. Isaac *(Genesis 22:6–13)*
305. Jesus *(Luke 2:7)*

Old and New Testament Prophets

306. Isaiah 53:12
307. Psalm 78:2
308. Micah 5:2
309. Zechariah 11:12
310. Psalm 22:18
311. Isaiah 53:7
312. Zechariah 9:9
313. Deuteronomy 18:18–22
314. Psalm 22:16
315. Isaiah 53:3
316. Isaiah 7:14

317. Hosea 11:1
318. Psalm 16:10
319. Isaiah 53:10
320. Zechariah 12:10
321. Elisha *(2 Kings 2–13)*
322. Amos *(Amos 5:24)*
323. Elijah *(1 Kings 17–2 Kings 2)*
324. Enoch *(Jude 14–15)*
325. Hosea *(Hosea 11:8–9)*
326. Ezekiel *(Ezekiel 4–5)*
327. Deborah *(Judges 4:4–9)*
328. Gad *(2 Samuel 24)*
329. Isaiah *(Isaiah 6:5–9)*
330. Huldah *(2 Chronicles 34)*
331. Zechariah *(Zechariah 8, 14)*
332. Joel *(Joel 2:28, 32)*
333. Jeremiah *(Jeremiah 13–17, 30–33)*
334. Jonah *(Jonah 3)*
335. Anna *(Luke 2:36–38)*
336. Amos *(Amos 7:14–15)*
337. Hosea *(Hosea 3:1)*
338. Zephaniah *(Zephaniah 1:7)*
339. Habakkuk *(Habakkuk 1:2)*
340. Nahum *(Nahum 2:6)*
341. Amos *(Amos 7:11)*
342. Jeremiah *(Jeremiah 51:33)*
343. Isaiah *(Isaiah 2:4)*

344. Daniel *(Daniel 5:26–28)*
345. Ezekiel *(Ezekiel 1:4)*
346. Haggai *(Haggai 1:6)*
347. Obadiah *(Obadiah 1:15)*
348. Amos *(Amos 9:11)*
349. Jonah *(Jonah 2:2)*
350. Zephaniah *(Zephaniah 2:13)*

Chapter 3—Living in Bible Times

Ritual and Worship

351. Pharisees *(Matthew 23:23–33)*
352. The stone tablets upon which God's covenant with the Hebrews is inscribed, a pot of manna, Aaron's rod, and the Books of the Law *(Exodus 37:1–8)*
353. On the seventh day of creation *(Genesis 2:2–3)*
354. Sadducees *(Matthew 22:23)*
355. Exodus 20:3–17
356. Passover *(Exodus 12:23–29)*
357. Synagogue *(Luke 4:16)*
358. Pentecost *(Acts 2:1–41)*
359. Sacrifice *(Exodus 5:17)*
360. Tabernacle *(Exodus 25:9)*
361. A rainbow *(Genesis 9:13)*
362. The Holy Spirit *(2 Corinthians 1:21)*

363. Solomon *(1 Kings 6:20)*
364. A divorced woman *(Ezekiel 44:22)*
365. Death *(Deuteronomy 17:12)*
366. Baal *and* the stars (*2 Kings 21:3–5*)
367. God and the Lamb *(Revelation 21:22)*
368. The names of the twelve tribes of Israel *(Exodus 28:21)*
369. Jesus *(Hebrews 3:1)*
370. Determining God's will *(Exodus 28:30)*
371. Circumcision *(Genesis 17:9–14)*
372. Building and worshiping the golden calf—a graven image *(Exodus 32)*
373. Aaron and his sons Nadab, Abihu, Eleazar, and Ithamar *(Exodus 28:1)*
374. Wine, which symbolizes the blood of sacrifice *(Mark 14:24)*
375. Baptism with water (immersion) *(Matthew 28:19)*

Home Sweet Home
376. Caves *(Judges 6:2)*
377. The roof *(Mark 2:3–4)*
378. The roof *(1 Samuel 9:25)*
379. Food, drink, and clothing *(Matthew 6:25–34)*
380. A bed, a table, a stool, and a candlestick *(2 Kings 4:10)*
381. A tent *(Genesis 18:1)*

382. The lamp *(Jeremiah 25:10)*
383. Eutychus *(Acts 20:9)*
384. Booths *(Nehemiah 8:14–16)*
385. An upstairs room *(Luke 22:11–12)*
386. Zacharias's and Elizabeth's *(Luke 1:39–41)*
387. The home of Mary and Martha *(Luke 10:38–42)*
388. Noah *(Genesis 9:21)*
389. Jonadab *(Jeremiah 35:6–10)*
390. Snakes *(Amos 5:19)*

Daily Chores

391. Niter (lye) and soap *(Jeremiah 2:22)*
392. Spinning cloth, including fine linen and mohair *(Exodus 35:25–26)*
393. Lemuel *(Proverbs 31:10–31)*
394. A needle *(Matthew 19:24)*
395. Oil *(Matthew 25:1–13)*

Pastimes and Play

396. Zechariah *(Zechariah 8:5)*
397. Music *(Psalm 68:25)*
398. Dice (casting lots) *(Mark 15:24)*
399. The timbrel or tambourine *(Exodus 15:20, Judges 11:34, Psalm 150:4, Jeremiah 31:4)*
400. Jesus *(Matthew 18:3)*

Burial and Mourning

401. Joseph of Arimathea *(Matthew 27:59–60)*

402. Ezekiel *(Ezekiel 24:15–18)*

403. Seven days *(Genesis 50:10)*

404. Thirty days *(Numbers 20:29)*

405. Joseph *(Genesis 50:4–6)*

406. The two prophets *(Revelation 11:3–9)*

407. Four days *(John 11:12)*

408. Aaron *(Leviticus 10:1–2, 6)*

409. A large stone *(Mark 15:46)*

410. They shall be comforted *(Matthew 5:4)*

411. Job *(Job 1:1–2, 18–20)*

412. The prophet Isaiah *(Isaiah 61:1–3)*

413. Poured expensive ointment (oil) over him *(Matthew 26:7–13)*

414. Rachel *(Genesis 35:16–20)*

415. Naomi *(Ruth 1:1-5, 20)*

Bible Occupations

416. Provincial rulers (appointed by Nebuchadnezzar) *(Daniel 2:49)*

417. Shepherdess *(Exodus 2:16–21)*

418. Guarding Paul *(Acts 27:1)*

419. Servant of Elisha *(2 Kings 4:12)*

420. Scribe *(Jeremiah 36:4)*

421. Tax collector *(Luke 19)*

422. Tentmakers *(Acts 18:3)*

423. A seller of purple cloth *(Acts 16:14)*
424. Thresher *(Judges 6:11)*
425. Fishermen *(Matthew 4:18–20)*

The Golden Years

426. Moses *(Deuteronomy 34:7)*
427. Caleb *(Joshua 14:7–12)*
428. Jacob *(Genesis 47:28–31)*
429. Methuselah *(Genesis 5:27)*
430. Elizabeth and Zacharias *(Luke 1:13–19)*
431. Shem *(Genesis 11:10–11)*
432. David *(1 Kings 1:1)*
433. Noah *(Genesis 7:6)*
434. Abraham *(Genesis 17:1, 5)*
435. Asa *(1 Kings 15:23)*

Buildings and Other Structures

436. They burned incense to idols *(Jeremiah 19:13)*
437. Omri *(1 Kings 16:23–24)*
438. Jabal *(Genesis 4:20)*
439. The temple *(Mark 13:1–2)*
440. Israelite slaves *(Exodus 1:11)*
441. The Samaritans *(2 Kings 7:3–16)*
442. Job *(Job 1:18–19)*
443. Ahasuerus *(Esther 1:5–6)*
444. Hiel *(1 Kings 16:3–4)*
445. Twelve *(Revelation 21:12)*

446. Pearl *(Revelation 21:21)*
447. Cain *(Genesis 4:17)*
448. Hiram *(2 Samuel 5:11)*
449. Nimrod *(Genesis 10:8–10)*
450. David's *(1 Samuel 17:54)*
451. The tabernacle *(Exodus 26:1–4)*
452. Damascus *(2 Corinthians 11:33)*
453. Joseph *(Genesis 37:22)*
454. The door of the ark *(Genesis 7:16)*
455. A tent *(Jeremiah 35:6–10)*

Clothing in Ancient Times

456. Purple *(Acts 16:14)*
457. Eye makeup *(Jeremiah 4:30, Ezekiel 23:40)*
458. Camel's hair *(Matthew 3:4)*
459. Gloves *(Genesis 27:16)*
460. Nothing *(2 Chronicles 28:15)*
461. Sandals *(Joshua 5:15)*
462. Veil *(Genesis 24:65)*
463. Linen *(Exodus 28:42)*
464. A coat of many colors *(Genesis 37:3)*
465. Fringed them and added blue ribbon
   (Numbers 15:38–39)

Money Earned, Money Spent

466. Genesis 23:13
467. Mark 6:8

468. Judges 16:18
469. Numbers 3:51
470. Matthew 17:21
471. Micah 3:11
472. Matthew 27:3
473. John 2:15
474. Lamentations 5:4
475. 2 Kings 15:20
476. 1 Timothy 6:10
477. Matthew 25:15
478. Leviticus 25:37
479. Matthew 25:25
480. Genesis 47:15

Food and Drink

481. Bread and lentil stew *(Genesis 25:34)*
482. Bread, meat, butter, and milk *(Genesis 18:6–8)*
483. Five loaves of bread and two fishes
     (Matthew 14:14–21)
484. Honey *(Judges 14:8)*
485. Broiled fish and honeycomb *(Luke 24:42)*
486. Wine *(Genesis 14:18)*
487. Grapes, pomegranates, and figs *(Numbers 13:23)*
488. Unleavened bread, meat, and broth
     (Judges 6:19–21)
489. Fish, cucumbers, melons, leeks, onions, and
     garlic *(Numbers 11:5)*

490. Manna *(Exodus 16:14–15)*

Flavorings, Spices, and Herbs

491. Salt *(Leviticus 2:13)*
492. Ezekiel *(Ezekiel 2:9–3:3)*
493. Mustard *(Matthew 13:31–32)*
494. John *(Revelation 10:9–10)*
495. Bitter herbs *(Exodus 12:8)*
496. The bread of deceit *(Proverbs 20:17)*
497. Poison *(Mark 16:17–18)*
498. Honey *(Matthew 3:4)*
499. Vinegar *(Matthew 27:48)*
500. He threw a tree into the waters. *(Exodus 15:25)*

Love, Marriage, and Family

501. The love of a mother for her child *(Isaiah 66:13)*
502. To teach his sons *(Proverbs 1:8)*
503. The Garden of Eden *(Genesis 2:23–25)*
504. Jesus *(Matthew 19:4-6, Mark 10:6–9)*
505. In their duty to God *(Deuteronomy 13:6–10)*
506. The love of God *(Matthew 22:37–38)*
507. Cana *(John 2:1–11)*
508. That a man lay down his life for his friends *(John 15:13)*
509. Love your neighbor as you would yourself. *(Leviticus 19:18)*

510. Paul *(Hebrews 13:4)*

Crime and Punishment

511. Micah *(Judges 17:1–4)*
512. Laban *(Genesis 29-31)*
513. The Spirit *(Matthew 10:16–20)*
514. Gezer *(1 Kings 9:16)*
515. One, the tribe of Judah *(2 Kings 17:18)*
516. Menahem *(2 Kings 15:14)*
517. Barabbas *(John 18:40)*
518. Joseph *(Genesis 39:7–20)*
519. Paul and Silas *(Acts 16:25–31)*
520. Absalom *(2 Samuel 13:37–38)*
521. Adam and Eve *(Genesis 3:22–24)*
522. Tiglath-pileser *(2 Kings 15:29)*
523. They were tried, beaten, and jailed. *(Acts 16:16–22)*
524. Two or three *(Deuteronomy 17:6)*
525. Samson *(Judges 16:24)*
526. John *(Revelation 1:9)*
527. The serpent *(Genesis 3:1–5)*
528. The chief priests *(Matthew 28:11–15)*
529. Death *(Leviticus 20:10)*
530. Hoshea *(2 Kings 17:4)*
531. Two *(Matthew 26:57–60)*
532. Cain *(Genesis 4:8)*
533. Festus, Agrippa, and Bernice *(Acts 25:23–26:32)*

534. Hagar and Ishmael *(Genesis 21:14)*
535. Samuel *(1 Samuel 8:1-3)*
536. His father-in-law Jethro *(Exodus 18:13–24)*
537. Cain *(Genesis 4:13–16)*
538. Nebuchadnezzar *(2 Kings 25:9)*
539. Zedekiah *(Jeremiah 52:11)*
540. Jeremiah *(Jeremiah 43:5–7)*
541. In the fields *(Genesis 4:8)*
542. The lords of the Philistines *(Judges 16:5)*
543. Judas *(John 12:4–6)*
544. Forty years *(Exodus 12:40)*
545. Absalom *(2 Samuel 14:28–33)*
546. John the Baptist *(Matthew 14:3–5)*
547. Moses *(Exodus 2:15)*
548. Absalom *(2 Samuel 15)*
549. Rachel *(Genesis 31:19)*
550. Benaiah *(1 Kings 2:29, 34)*
551. The priests saw with their own eyes the lame man whom Peter and John had healed. *(Acts 4:14)*
552. Jehu *(2 Kings 9)*
553. Amalekites *(1 Samuel 30:1)*
554. Joseph *(Genesis 42)*
555. Abimelech *(Judges 9:49)*
556. Hanani *(2 Chronicles 16:10)*
557. Hoshea *(2 Kings 15:30)*
558. Zedekiah *(2 Kings 25:6–7)*

559. Bathsheba *(2 Samuel 11)*
560. Peter and John *(Acts 4:3)*

Chapter 4—Bible Geography

Mountainous Country

561. Moriah *(Genesis 22:2)*
562. Tabor *(Judges 4:6–15)*
563. Gilboa *(1 Samuel 31:1–6)*
564. Pisgah *(Deuteronomy 34:5–6)*
565. Carmel *(1 Kings 18:29)*
566. The Mount of Olives *(Luke 19:37–41)*
567. Horeb *(Exodus 17:6)*
568. Sinai *(Exodus 31:18)*
569. Ararat *(Genesis 8:4)*
570. Nebo *(Deuteronomy 34:1–4)*

Cities and Fortresses

571. The New Jerusalem *(Revelation 21:18)*
572. Gilgal *(1 Samuel 11:14–15)*
573. Bethsaida *(John 1)*
574. Tarshish *(Jonah 1:3)*
575. Jerusalem *(1 Kings 9:15)*
576. Damascus *(2 Kings 8:7)*
577. Nain *(Luke 7:11–15)*
578. Philadelphia *(Revelation 3:7–13)*

579. Shiloh *(Joshua 18:1)*
580. Megiddo *(2 Kings 23:9)*
581. Berea *(Acts 17:10–14)*
582. Jericho *(Joshua 6)*
583. Succoth *(Judges 8:5–16)*
584. Babylon *(2 Kings 25)*
585. Tarsus *(Acts 21:39)*
586. Gath *(1 Samuel 17:4)*
587. Jericho *(Luke 19:1)*
588. Antioch *(Acts 11:26)*
589. Ekron *(2 Kings 1:2)*
590. Jerusalem *(2 Kings 25:10)*

Bodies of Water

591. The Red Sea *(Exodus 15:4)*
592. The Sea of Galilee *(John 6, Matthew 4)*
593. Ahava *(Ezra 8:21)*
594. Egypt *(Exodus 7:14–19)*
595. The Jordan *(2 Kings 5:10–14)*
596. The Salt Sea *(Genesis 14:3)*
597. Kerith Brook *(1 Kings 17:1–4)*
598. The Sea of Tiberias *(John 21:1)*
599. Gihon, Pison, Tigris, and Euphrates *(Genesis 2:10–14)*
600. The Jordan *(Mark 1:5)*

Deserts and Plains

601. Exodus *(Exodus 5:3)*
602. 1 Samuel *(1 Samuel 10:3)*
603. Matthew *(Matthew 14:13)*
604. Genesis *(Genesis 12:6)*
605. Luke *(Luke 1:80)*

Islands and Oases

606. Revelation *(Revelation 1:9)*
607. Isaiah *(Isaiah 51:3)*
608. Numbers *(Numbers 20:11)*
609. Acts of the Apostles *(Acts 28:1–2)*
610. Isaiah *(Isaiah 35:6–7)*

Valleys

611. Megiddo *(2 Chronicles 35:22–24)*
612. Elah *(1 Samuel 17:19, 49)*
613. Berachah *(2 Chronicles 20:25–26)*
614. Jehoshaphat *(Joel 3:2)*
615. Hinnom *(2 Chronicles 28:1–3)*

Biblical Travels

616. Joseph *(Matthew 2:19–21)*
617. Moses *(Deuteronomy 32:49–52)*
618. Elisha *(2 Kings 2:2–7)*
619. Ruth *(Ruth 1:18–19)*

620. Wise men *(Matthew 2:1)*
621. Jacob's sons *(Genesis 42:2–3)*
622. The disciples *(Luke 9:1–3)*
623. Jonah *(Jonah 1:1–2)*
624. Rebekah *(Genesis 24:58–61)*
625. Barnabus *(Acts 13:2–4)*

Chapter 5—The Natural World in Bible Times

Fishes Great and Small

626. Four: Simon Peter, Andrew, James, and John *(Matthew 4:18–21)*
627. Man *(Genesis 1:26)*
628. Three days and three nights *(Jonah 1:17)*
629. The water turned to blood. *(Exodus 7:17–18)*
630. Simon and Andrew *(Mark 1:16–17)*
631. Noah *(Genesis 2:1–2)*
632. A "piece of money" *(Matthew 17:27)*
633. An evil time *(Ecclesiastes 9:12)*
634. Jesus *(Matthew 7:9–10)*
635. Solomon *(1 Kings 4:30–33)*

The Birds and the Beasts

636. Balaam *(Numbers 22:21–33)*
637. David *(1 Samuel 7:34–36)*
638. Quail *(Exodus 16:12–13)*

639. In the temple *(John 2:13–14)*
640. Camel *(Genesis 24:64)*
641. Oxen *(Job 1:14)*
642. Abel *(Genesis 4:2)*
643. Calf *(Exodus 32:4)*
644. The disciples *(Matthew 10:16)*
645. Dove *(Genesis 8:8)*
646. Cock *(Matthew 26:34)*
647. Lamb *(Exodus 12:3–13)*
648. Ass *(Matthew 21:5)*
649. Samson *(Judges 15:4–5)*
650. The poor man *(2 Samuel 12:3)*

Reptiles, Insects, and Amphibians

651. Locusts *(Exodus 10:4–6)*
652. Serpent *(Genesis 3:1–6)*
653. Ants, locusts, rock badgers, and spiders *(Proverbs 30:24–28)*
654. Lizard *(Leviticus 11:30)*
655. Fly *(Exodus 8:21)*
656. John the Baptist *(Mark 1:6)*
657. Viper *(Acts 28:1–6)*
658. A swarm of bees *(Judges 14:8)*
659. Locusts *(Revelation 9:9)*
660. Frogs *(Exodus 8:2)*

All That Glitters

661. Twelve *(Exodus 28:17–20)*
662. Lips of knowledge *(Proverbs 20:15)*
663. Golden earrings *(Judges 8:24)*
664. Pearl *(Matthew 14:45–46)*
665. To make an offering to the tabernacle *(Exodus 35:22)*
666. Onyx *(1 Chronicles 29:2)*
667. God *(Isaiah 54:11–12)*
668. A heavenly throne *(Revelation 4:2–3)*
669. Rubies *(Job 28:18)*
670. Golden earrings and bracelets *(Genesis 24:22)*
671. Those who fear the Lord *(Malachi 3:16–17)*
672. The prodigal son *(Luke 15:22)*
673. Earring *(Proverbs 25:12)*
674. Jehoshaphat *(2 Chronicles 20:25)*
675. Pharaoh *(Genesis 41:42)*

Sun, Moon, and Stars

676. Jesus *(Revelation 22:16)*
677. The moon *(Genesis 1:16)*
678. Abram's descendants *(Genesis 15:5)*
679. Job *(Job 38:31–33)*
680. Worshiping the sun *(Ezekiel 8:16)*
681. Astrologers *(Daniel 2:2)*
682. God *(Psalm 147:4)*

683. Worship of the sun, moon, planets, and stars *(2 Kings 23:4–5)*
684. A star *(Matthew 2:2)*
685. To divide day from night; for signs; to count seasons, days, and years *(Genesis 1:14)*

Fire and Ice

686. Sodom and Gomorrah *(Genesis 19:24)*
687. A pillar of fire *(Exodus 14:24)*
688. Job *(Job 6:16)*
689. Honor is not seemly for a fool *(Proverbs 26:1)*
690. Manna *(Exodus 16:14–15)*
691. An angel *(Revelation 10:1)*
692. Kindled a fire *(Acts 28:1–2)*
693. James *(James 1:11)*
694. Those who do not abide in the Lord *(John 15:6)*
695. He made a burnt offering *(Genesis 8:21)*

The Bible Rainbow

696. Purple *(Acts 16:14)*
697. Blue *(Ezekiel 23:6)*
698. A plague of leprosy *(Leviticus 13:49)*
699. White *(Revelation 6:2)*
700. Green *(Psalm 23:2)*
701. The Red Sea *(Exodus 15:22)*
702. Those who sat in judgment *(Judges 5:10)*

703. Purple *(Mark 15:17)*
704. Fir tree *(Hosea 14:8)*
705. Black *(Revelation 6:5)*
706. Blue and white *(Esther 9:15)*
707. Coat of many colors *(Genesis 37:3–4)*
708. A scale *(Revelation 6:5)*
709. They saw Moses and Elias (Elijah) talking with him *(Matthew 17:1–3)*
710. A rainbow—his "bow in the cloud" *(Genesis 9:13)*

Trees, Plants, and Crops

711. Hyssop *(Psalm 51:7)*
712. Reed *(Mark 15:19)*
713. Jericho *(2 Chronicles 28:15)*
714. Gourd *(Jonah 4:6)*
715. Olive *(Genesis 8:11)*
716. Song of Solomon *(Song of Solomon 2:3)*
717. Wormwood *(Lamentations 3:15, Amos 5:7)*
718. Mustard *(Matthew 13:13–32)*
719. The ark *(Genesis 6:14)*
720. Fig *(Mark 11:12–14)*
721. Thorns *(Matthew 13:7)*
722. The third day *(Genesis 1:9–13)*
723. Wheat and rye *(Exodus 9:32)*
724. Almond *(Jeremiah 1:11)*
725. Juniper *(1 Kings 19:4–5)*

Chapter 6—Bible History and Epic

In the Beginning

726. The spirit of God *(Genesis 1:2)*
727. By blocking their way with angels and a flaming sword *(Genesis 3:24)*
728. Adam *(Genesis 2:19)*
729. To crawl on its belly and be despised *(Genesis 3:14)*
730. By causing a mist to rise up from the earth *(Genesis 2:6)*
731. The tree of knowledge of good and evil *(Genesis 2:17)*
732. God breathed into his nostrils. *(Genesis 2:7)*
733. Pain in childbirth, earning a living from working the earth *(Genesis 3:16–23)*
734. It meant, "taken out of man." *(Genesis 2:23)*
735. They hid. *(Genesis 3:8)*
736. Dust of the earth *(Genesis 2:7)*
737. The lights in the sky *(Genesis 1:14–19)*
738. In the east *(Genesis 2:8)*
739. Fruit *(Genesis 1:29)*
740. Heaven *(Genesis 1:7–8)*

Biblical Battles

741. An angel of the Lord *(2 Kings 19:35)*
742. Because they had forsaken the Lord *(2 Chronicles 28:6)*

743. The prayer of Elisha *(2 Kings 6:18–23)*
744. Egypt *(Exodus 14:13–31)*
745. Hailstones *(Joshua 10:6–13)*
746. Jesus *(Matthew 10:34)*
747. 120,000 *(Judges 8:10)*
748. Ben-hadad *(1 Kings 20:29–30)*
749. Syrians *(1 Chronicles 19:18)*
750. Abijah *(2 Chronicles 13:17)*
751. Three unclean spirits *(Revelation 16:14)*
752. Moses' arms were held aloft. *(Exodus 17:11)*
753. He had his people sing praises unto the Lord. *(2 Chronicles 20:22)*
754. Eli *(1 Samuel 4:13–18)*
755. David *(1 Chronicles 20:18)*

The Gospel of Jesus

756. An angel *(Luke 2:8–11)*
757. To pay a tribute *(Matthew 17:24–27)*
758. Soldiers cast lots for it. *(John 19:23–24)*
759. Mary Magdalene *(John 20:15)*
760. He raised her son from the dead. *(Luke 7:11)*
761. Jesus *(John 13:5)*
762. God warned them in a dream. *(Matthew 2:12)*
763. Cæsar Augustus *(Luke 2:1)*
764. An angel *(Matthew 3:13)*
765. With a kiss *(Luke 22:47)*

766. Having dinner at the home of Simon the leper *(Matthew 26:6–7)*

767. They slept. *(Mark 14:32–42)*

768. His mother *(John 2:1–11)*

769. Peter *(Matthew 14:25–31)*

770. Joseph of Arimathea and Nicodemus *(John 19:38–39)*

771. Bought a field to be used as a graveyard *(Matthew 27:3–8)*

772. Simon of Cyrene *(Mark 15:21)*

773. Mary and Mary Magdalene *(Matthew 27:55–56)*

774. He said Jesus had "committed no crime." *(John 19:6)*

775. He was hoping to see a miracle. *(Luke 23:8)*

Bible Family Trees

776. David *(Matthew 1:6–16)*

777. Moses *(Exodus 7:7)*

778. Zebedee *(Mark 1:19–20)*

779. Ham *(Genesis 9:18)*

780. Eve *(Genesis 3:20)*

781. John the Baptist *(Luke 1:5–15, Matthew 3:1)*

782. Kish *(1 Samuel 9:1–2)*

783. Obed *(Matthew 1:6)*

784. Esau *(Genesis 25:28)*

785. Seven sons, three daughters *(Job 42:12–13)*

The Early Church

786. Epaphras *(Colossians 1:7)*
787. Philippi *(Philippians 2:25)*
788. Timothy (Timotheus) *(Acts 16:3)*
789. Priscilla and Aquila *(Acts 18:2)*
790. Matthias *(Acts 1:26)*
791. Saul *(Acts 9:1–3)*
792. Antioch of Pisidia *(Acts 13:16)*
793. James *(Acts 15:13)*
794. Ananias *(Acts 9:10–18)*
795. Dorcas *(Acts 9:36)*

Religious Journeys and Retreats

796. Horeb *(Exodus 3:1–4)*
797. John the Baptist *(Matthew 3:1–3)*
798. The death of Herod *(Matthew 2:19–23)*
799. The wilderness *(Matthew 4:1–2)*
800. Daniel *(Daniel 10:1–3)*
801. Bethel *(2 Kings 2:2)*
802. The Lord *(Psalm 9:9)*
803. The word of the Lord *(Amos 9:11–12)*
804. Forty days and forty nights *(Exodus 34:28)*
805. John *(Book of Revelation)*

Biblical Proportions

806. 300 cubits long, 50 cubits wide, and 30 cubits high *(Genesis 6:15)*

807. 12,000 furlongs square *(Revelation 21:16)*
808. 50 cubits *(Esther 5:18)*
809. Two-and-a-half cubits long, a cubit and a half wide, and a cubit and a half high *(Exodus 37:1)*
810. 144 cubits *(Revelation 21:17)*

Dreams and Visions

811. Daniel *(Daniel 7:2)*
812. Joseph *(Genesis 37:9)*
813. Stephen *(Acts 7:54–59)*
814. Ezekiel *(Ezekiel 37:1–2)*
815. Jacob *(Genesis 28:10–12)*
816. Job *(Job 7:14)*
817. Belshazzar *(Daniel 5:1–5)*
818. Nebuchadnezzar *(Daniel 4:1–11)*
819. Pharaoh *(Genesis 41:17–19)*
820. John *(Revelation 5:1)*

Prophecies About the Messiah Fulfilled

821. "Judas Iscariot went unto the chief priests, and said unto them, What will ye give me, and I will deliver him unto you? And they covenanted with him for thirty pieces of silver." *(Matthew 26:14–15)*
822. "...They parted his garments, casting lots upon them ...." *(Mark 15:24)*

823. "... For that which is conceived in her is of the Holy Ghost." *(Matthew 2:20–21)*

824. "But when they came to Jesus ... they brake not his legs." *(John 19:32–33)*

825. "And he spake also a parable unto them...." *(Luke 5:36)*

826. "And when they drew nigh unto Jerusalem ... the disciples ... brought an ass ... and they set him thereon ..." *(Matthew 21:1–11)*

827. "But one of the soldiers with a spear pierced his side..." *(John 19:34)*

828. "And the soldiers also mocked him, coming to him, and offering him vinegar." *(Luke 23:36)*

829. "But when Herod was dead, behold, an angel of the Lord appeareth in a dream to Joseph in Egypt, saying Arise, and take the young child and his mother, and go into the land of Israel." *(Matthew 2:19–20)*

830. "Then there were two thieves crucified with him, one on the right hand, and another on the left." *(Matthew 27:38)*

Favorite Bible Stories

831. One *(Genesis 11:1)*

832. Because Pharaoh had ordered the killing of all newborn Hebrew sons *(Exodus 1:16-22)*

833. To shout *(Joshua 6:16)*

834. Boaz *(Ruth 4:13)*
835. Because he was a Nazarite, and it was customary for Nazarites to wear their hair long. *(Judges 16:17)*
836. His sister Miriam *(Exodus 2:4)*
837. They took it to their father. *(Genesis 37:22)*
838. An angel *(Genesis 22:10–12)*
839. Jesus' birth *(Luke 2:14)*
840. He was to bring food and water to his brothers in battle. *(1 Samuel 17:17–18)*
841. He built an altar to worship God. *(Genesis 9:20)*
842. Darius *(Daniel 6:1–16)*
843. Gennesaret *(Luke 5:1–6)*
844. He asked to be made one of his father's "hired men." *(Luke 15:19)*
845. Jacob *(Genesis 33:24-28)*

Chapter 7—Bible Inspiration

Jesus' Teachings

846. Shake the dust from their feet *(Mark 6:11)*
847. By being born of the Spirit *(John 3:5–7)*
848. False prophets *(Matthew 7:15)*
849. With God *(Luke 18:27)*
850. "Render to Cæsar the things that are Cæsar's, and to God the things that are God's." *(Mark 12:17)*

851. "That ye love one another; as I have loved you, that ye also love one another." *(John 13:34)*
852. Mercy in return *(Matthew 5:7)*
853. "To seek and to save that which was lost" *Luke 19:10)*
854. "The kingdom of heaven is at hand." *(Matthew 10:7)*
855. Sinners *(Matthew 9:13)*
856. Jesus will bring them to everlasting life. *(John 6:40)*
857. Shall not stand *(Matthew 12:24)*
858. A camel to go through a needle's eye *(Luke 18:25)*
859. And lose his own soul *(Mark 8:36)*
860. Serpents *and* doves *(Matthew 10:16)*

The Book of Psalms

861. Acts 13:33
862. Psalm 51
863. Psalm 8:2
864. Thunder *(Psalm 29:3)*
865. Psalm 22:1
866. Moses
867. Psalm 18:2
868. Psalm 65:12–13
869. Trumpet, psaltery, harp, timbrel, stringed instruments, organ, cymbals *(Psalm 150:3-5)*

870. Psalm 100
871. Psalm 114:4
872. Those who are upright, righteous, and truthful
    (Psalm 15:2)
873. Psalm 73
874. Psalm 126:5
875. Psalm 27

Wise Proverbs

876. Wrath *(Proverbs 15:1)*
877. A merry heart *(Proverbs 17:22)*
878. Rod *(Proverbs 13:24)*
879. Righteousness *(Proverbs 15:9)*
880. Ant *(Proverbs 6:6)*
881. Praise *(Proverbs 27:2)*
882. Apples *(Proverbs 25:11)*
883. Labor *(Proverbs 13:11)*
884. Maketh it glad *(Proverbs 12:25)*
885. Trust *(Proverbs 3:5)*

The Parables of Jesus

886. A priest and a Levite *(Luke 10:30–33)*
887. He went to find it. *(Matthew 18:12–13; Luke 15:4–6)*
888. "The last shall be first, and the first last" *(Matthew 20:1–16)*
889. The father of the prodigal son *(Luke 15:11–32)*

890. The ten virgins *(Matthew 25:1–13)*
891. People who took Jesus' teachings to heart.
(Matthew 13:3–8; Mark 4:3–8; Luke 8:5–8)
892. The pharisee and the publican *(Luke 18:10–14)*
893. The friend who asked to borrow bread
(Luke 11:5–8)
894. The wedding feast *(Matthew 22:2–14)*
895. A fig tree *(Luke 13:6–9)*

Ecclesiastes and the Song of Solomon

896. The Song of Songs *(Song of Solomon 1:1)*
897. A time to every purpose under heaven
(Ecclesiastes 3:1)
898. Spices, honeycomb, milk, and honey
(Song of Solomon 5:1)
899. Precious ointment *(Ecclesiastes 7:1)*
900. The Preacher, the son of David *(Ecclesiastes 1:1)*
901. Springtime *(Song of Solomon 2:1–17)*
902. The earth *(Ecclesiastes 1:4)*
903. King Solomon *(Song of Solomon 3:11)*
904. A lily among thorns *(Song of Solomon 2:2)*
905. Laugh *and* dance *(Ecclesiastes 3:4)*

Faith, Hope, and Charity

906. Charity *(1 Corinthians 13:13)*
907. Faith in God *(Mark 11:22–23)*
908. Psalms *(Psalm 146:5)*

909. James *(James 5:15)*
910. Jesus *(Revelation 2:19)*
911. 1 Thessalonians *(1 Thessalonians 5:8)*
912. The Lord's compassion *(Lamentations 3:19–22)*
913. Good works *(James 2:22)*
914. Paul *(1 Corinthians 13:4)*
915. Habakkuk *(Habakkuk 2:4)*

It's a Miracle

916. It budded, blossomed, and yielded almonds.
     (Numbers 17:8)
917. The sun and the moon stood still.
     (Joshua 10:12–14)
918. Tell anyone *(Matthew 9:27–31)*
919. Peter *(Matthew 14:28–31)*
920. Quail *(Exodus 16:11–13)*
921. The Shunammite woman's son
     (2 Kings 4:32–37)
922. She touched the hem of Jesus' garment.
     (Matthew 9:20–22)
923. Wash in the Jordan River seven times
     (2 Kings 5:10)
924. Moses' *(Exodus 9:22–26)*
925. Aeneas *(Acts 9:33–34)*
926. Locked doors *(John 20:19–21)*
927. He turned water into wine. *(John 2:1–11)*
928. Paul *(Acts 20:9–10)*

929. By Moses placing a brass serpent on a pole
     (Numbers 21:5–9)
930. Moses and Elijah *(Luke 9:28–36)*
931. Aaron's *(Exodus 7:10–12)*
932. They spoke in tongues. *(Acts 19:1–7)*
933. He was sleeping. *(Matthew 8:23–27)*
934. Because it was the Sabbath *(Luke 13:11–13)*
935. He made the wheels come off.
     (Exodus 14:23–25)
936. He touched her hand. *(Matthew 8:14–15)*
937. Dorcas *(Acts 9:36–41)*
938. Capernaum *(Luke 4:31–37)*
939. Bethany *(John 11)*
940. It came back to life. *(2 Kings 13:20–21)*

Heavenly Messengers

941. The captain of the Lord's host *(Joshua 5:13–14)*
942. Philip *(Acts 8:26)*
943. Samson *(Judges 13:11–20)*
944. Cherubim *(Genesis 3:24)*
945. John the Baptist *(Luke 1:13)*
946. Gabriel *(Luke 1:5–38)*
947. Elijah *(1 Kings 19:5–6)*
948. Abraham *(Genesis 22:11–18)*
949. Seraphim *(Isaiah 6:1–6)*
950. Two *(Genesis 19:1–22)*
951. Gethsemane *(Luke 22:43)*

952. Gabriel *(Daniel 8:15–16)*
953. A chain *(Revelation 20:2)*
954. Zechariah *(Zechariah 1:8)*
955. Twelve *(Revelation 21:12)*

Letters and Epistles

956. Sennacherib *(2 Kings 19:14)*
957. Paul *(Romans 11:13–14)*
958. Jesus *(Revelation 1–3)*
959. Claudius Lysias *(Acts 23:25–26)*
960. Elijah *(2 Chronicles 21:12)*
961. Paul and Sosthenes *(1 Corinthians 1:1)*
962. Naaman *(2 Kings 5:5–6)*
963. Colossians *(Colossians 4:16)*
964. Paul *(Philemon)*
965. To send Bathsheba's husband Uriah into battle
    (2 Samuel 11:4, 15)
966. Jezebel *(1 Kings 21:7–10)*
967. The Ephesians *(Acts 18:24–19:1)*
968. Peter *(1 Peter 1:1)*
969. Paul *(Acts 9:2)*
970. Jehu *(2 Kings 10:1–7)*

Praise and Prayer

971. David *(Psalm 55:17)*
972. Stephen *(Acts 7:59–60)*
973. Abraham *(Genesis 15:1–3)*

974. Mary *(Luke 1:46–49)*
975. Jesus *(John 17:1)*
976. Moses *(Exodus 33:18)*
977. The thief on the cross *(Luke 23:42)*
978. Paul and Silas *(Acts 16:25–26)*
979. Hezekiah *(2 Kings 19:14–16)*
980. Jonah *(Jonah 2:4)*
981. Jesus *(Matthew 6:11–12)*
982. David *(Psalm 31:3–4)*
983. Hannah *(1 Samuel 1:27–28)*
984. Jesus *(Matthew 26:42)*
985. Paul *(2 Corinthians 12:7–8)*
986. Elijah *(1 Kings 18:37–38)*
987. Peter *(Acts 10:40)*
988. David *(2 Samuel 24:10)*
989. Job *(Job 43:6)*
990. Moses and the Israelites *(Exodus 15:11)*

Bible Promises and Covenants

991. It shall be done unto you *(John 15:7)*
992. Bow *(Genesis 9:13)*
993. Land *(Exodus 6:8)*
994. Whatsoever she would ask *(Matthew 14:6–7)*
995. Many nations *(Genesis 17:4)*
996. Paradise *(Luke 23:43)*

997. Ten Commandments *(Deuteronomy 4:13)*
998. Children of God *(Matthew 5:9)*
999. John *(Luke 1:13)*
1000. Saved *(Mark 16:16)*

About the Author

Cathy Drinkwater Better is a professional writer and editor. Her articles, poetry, and humor for both children and adults have appeared internationally in magazines and journals since 1976. Currently an editor for a Baltimore-area book publisher, she worked for many years as a newspaper reporter, features writer, and photographer. An award-winning humorist and the author of several adult and children's books, she writes a monthly column for a family magazine.

Better also teaches creative writing for adults, and has led writing workshops in the schools. A martial arts instructor for all ages, she holds a 2nd-degree black belt in karate and teaches t'ai chi ch'uan.

Better has always been fascinated by world religions, and is a lifelong student of the Bible. She lives in Maryland, surrounded by books.